Introduction

100% Practical Ideas, Information, Strategies for K–6 Teachers is written with today's busy teacher in mind. The ideas are 100% practical, interesting to students, and easy for teachers to implement. You do not have to buy special products or spend your valuable time making materials. I've included so much information that will help you be a more effective teacher who works smarter, not harder.

This book contains a wealth of ideas and covers many topics. As you go through it, underline or highlight ideas you plan to use. As you read, jot down ideas that pop into your head in the spaces provided on the pages and notes at the end of each chapter. Keep this book handy—you'll use it all year long.

100% Practical will help you

- create active readers, writers, and thinkers

- organize your instructional program and the learning day

- provide up-to-date, educationally sound strategies to help students achieve excellence

Barbara Gruber

Barbara Gruber, M.A.

Written by Barbara Gruber, M.A.
Illustrated by Lynn Conklin Power, Leslie Franz and Becky Radtke
FS-8128 100% Practical
All rights reserved—Printed in the U.S.A.
Copyright © 1993 Frank Schaffer Publications, Inc.
23740 Hawthorne Blvd.
Torrance, CA 90505

Table of Contents

You're the Expert in Your Classroom!

Every teacher has a personal style and specific beliefs about the ways children learn. And every teacher has preferred ways for managing and organizing his or her classroom.

Ideally, teachers remain receptive to new ideas and changes in education throughout their careers. By reading, attending conferences, and talking with colleagues, they learn about new trends. Then, while maintaining their personal styles, they can decide how to adapt and implement new strategies into their classrooms.

Teaching styles can be as unique as the teachers themselves.

Every teacher is an expert about what is best for his or her students and classroom. Individual teachers are the only ones who can know what will and won't work for them and their students.

The whole-language philosophy provides many strategies teachers can use to improve their programs. In my view, there are many valid ways to implement the whole-language philosophy.

Teachers know what is best for their own students and classrooms.

When teachers are empowered to make decisions and believe in the ways they are teaching, enthusiasm and motivation are heightened. When teachers are enthusiastic about teaching and learning, students are motivated, eager learners. The whole-language philosophy gives teachers opportunities and strategies to enrich the learning day.

Where Does Whole Language Fit In?

Theories and practices in education are always changing. Some ideas seem to come and go, only to return again bearing a new name. I have the pleasure of working with thousands of teachers each school year through seminars and as an author. Based on my observations and contacts with educators, I believe the movement toward whole language has caused more anxiety, debate, and polarization than other changes and trends in education. The whole-language philosophy is embraced and interpreted in many different ways.

Beliefs seem to range from a "purist" to a "conservative" viewpoint. Purists tend to feel that literature, not basals, should be the sole basis for reading. Conservatives tend to believe that basals can be integrated into a whole-language classroom.

My own beliefs about whole language, learning, and classroom teaching tend to lean toward the conservative point of view. The questions on the following pages are those I encounter most about whole language and teaching in the 1990s. The answers reflect my personal views.

There are many ways to implement whole language successfully.

1. What is whole language?

Rather than being a teaching method or program with a precise definition, whole language is more of a philosophy or a viewpoint. Because of this, it means different things to different people. There is no single, correct way to interpret and implement whole language. However, the following points are generally accepted as basic tenets of the whole-language philosophy:

- A child's literacy develops early in life.
- Using language is the best way to develop language competency.
- Language should be used in functional, meaningful, purposeful ways.
- Skills are taught in context with focus on meaning.
- Speaking, listening, reading and writing are linked.

Whole language is a philosophy, not a teaching method.

2. Do teachers have to change the way they teach?

Absolutely not! Many classroom activities teachers have used over the years belong in today's whole-language classrooms. Here are a few examples:

- using literature
- reading aloud to students
- sustained silent reading
- classroom publishing
- journal writing
- linking reading, writing, listening, and speaking
- integrating the curriculum/the thematic approach

Whole language can be a part of many different teaching styles.

> *All reading materials can have a place in a whole-language classroom.*

3. Is it OK to use basal readers?

Yes! It is how the reading material is being used, rather than the source of the story, that is the most significant factor. It is possible to use literature exclusively and not have a whole-language approach. For example, you could use literature, teach skills in isolation, and follow up with lots of workbook pages.

Conversely, you can use a basal-reader story, teach skills in context, and link related oral- and written-language activities, and you would certainly be using a whole-language approach even though you are not using literature as your base.

No one questions the importance of exposing students to a wealth of children's literature. This can be done through the books you read aloud and books students read.

4. What about teaching skills?

Skills need to be taught in context. Teachers are held responsible for students' growth and progress from the beginning to the end of the year. Students deserve to be taught the skills that are appropriate for their grade levels. I think it is dangerous to assume that all skills are being covered by simply doing a lot of reading and writing.

> *Skills are best learned in context.*

To make sure appropriate skills are introduced and reinforced I recommend making a skills chart. At a glance, teachers can determine which skill they can introduce or reinforce in the context of the learning activity.

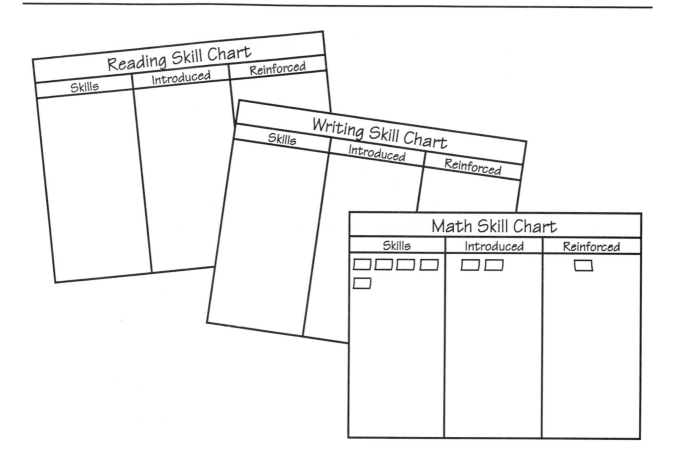

Reading Skill Chart

Skills	Introduced	Reinforced

Writing Skill Chart

Skills	Introduced	Reinforced

Math Skill Chart

Skills	Introduced	Reinforced
▢ ▢ ▢ ▢ ▢	▢ ▢	▢

To make a skills chart for reading, simply write each skill you need to cover on a stick-on note. Then, at the beginning of the year, post those notes on the chart under "Skills." If you do a shared-reading activity with your class that lends itself to a lesson on plurals, use words from the poem or story to teach about plurals. Then take the stick-on note for plurals and move it over to the "Introduced" column. When you reinforce that lesson on plurals at another time, move the stick-on note over to the "Reinforced" column. The goal is to get all skills moved across the chart and then to reinforce those skills in context. You can also use this method for tracking skills in other subjects, such as writing and mathematics.

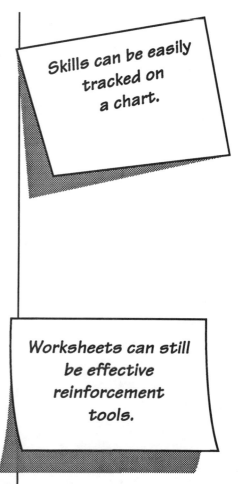

Skills can be easily tracked on a chart.

5. Can you use worksheet activities?

Yes! If you have taught a lesson on plurals using words from a shared-reading activity, you can have students do a paper and pencil activity that focuses on plurals. The worksheet provides reinforcement for the skill taught in context.

Worksheets can still be effective reinforcement tools.

> *Flexible grouping can help you reach and teach every child.*

6. What about grouping students?

An instructional program should have a balance of whole-class, small-group, partner, and individual activities.

There is a trend in the 90s to keep the whole class together for reading instruction. Many reading programs suggest treating the whole class as one group and having students all read the same material.

For some reading activities, such as shared reading, this is a good idea. However, it is my view that flexible grouping, in which students read material at their particular instructional levels, is most appropriate for the core instructional reading program.

It concerns me to have capable readers always reading material that is not challenging to them and carrying along students for whom the material may be too difficult.

I do not recommend consistently using the same material with the weakest and the strongest readers in the class because the gap between student skills is too great. This gap often widens even further as students progress through the grades. For these reasons, I believe in flexible grouping at all grade levels.

We have all heard and read suggestions about having capable readers paired up with less-capable readers. I believe reading-partner activities have a valuable place in classrooms; however, all students should be gaining new skills and reading material that is appropriate for them.

> *Strong and weak readers have different needs.*

7. Do whole-language teachers need to buy or make a lot of special materials?

No. You want to provide a wealth of reading and writing activities, but the essential elements are simply stories to read and paper for writing and making charts.

8. Do teachers need to spend a lot of time preparing for whole language?

It depends how you choose to approach it. I know a teacher who spent most of the summer making charts, sentence strips about literature, and word cards. For example, she wrote sentences about *Sylvester and the Magic Pebble* on sentence strips to use later for a sequencing activity.

This teacher could have saved herself time and made the activity more relevant and valuable to the children by reading the book aloud to students and eliciting sentences about the story from them. She could then have printed the sentences on sentence strips as students dictated them.

An activity performed with students during class time, rather than one prepared for them, has these advantages:

- Students connect reading, writing, and speaking.
- Students' actual language is recorded on the strips.
- Students develop a sense of shared responsibility and participation.
- The lesson is more flexible and relevant.
- The teacher's time is saved by elimating unneccesary preparation.

9. What about teaching phonics?

The purpose of reading is to gain meaning from the printed text. Phonics instruction is an important facet of reading instruction. Working with invented spellings and word families helps students acquire a knowledge of sound-symbol correspondence. Phonics is one of the important tools utilized by skillful readers.

Phonics remains a powerful reading tool.

10. What is the best way to implement the whole-language philosophy?

Teachers should implement changes gradually, one step at a time. When teachers make small changes, they can take time to focus on the ramifications of the change, then make further changes based on their experiences. When too many things are altered simultaneously, it is difficult to pinpoint what is and isn't working. Rapid, drastic change is stressful and difficult for teachers and students. One way to begin is by asking yourself which aspects of your current program you feel should stay the same and which can be adapted to fit the modications you are considering.

Make changes slowly ... one step at a time.

11. What about those who say using basals or teaching phonics is "old-fashioned"?

Teachers need to do what they feel is best in their classrooms. To be effective, they must believe in themselves and the way they teach. People who label others according to their educational beliefs are missing the whole point of teacher empowerment. There is more than one way to incorporate the whole-language philosophy. For many teachers, it can include teaching phonics in context and using basals.

A teacher's goal is to be effective.

12. How can a sense of community be established in a classroom?

Begin on the first day of school to set an atmosphere of ownership, community, and shared responsibility. Show the students that it is their classroom, not just yours. The following are some ways a teacher can develop a sense of community in the classroom:

- Say "our classroom, our books, our materials, our desks, our rules and agreements," instead of "my" classroom, etc.

- Inform students that their job is to prepare themselves for next grade. Many students think of this as the teacher's responsibility. Explain that your job, as the teacher, is to help students succeed at preparing themselves for the next grade level.

- Instead of doing things for students, do things with them. Rather than creating teacher-made bulletin boards, involve students in making bulletin boards that belong to the class.

- Allow students to make decisions about some aspects of their learning. Many of the learning activities in this book encourage students to make choices.

- Have a balanced program that includes individual, partner, small-group, and class activities.

- Encourage students to help each other.

- Ask the class for its input or to help you. Say "What do you think might be a good way to . . . " or "I'd like some help from you on how we can . . ."

- Have students give input on how desks and tables should be arranged in their classroom.

- Hold class discussions that help children develop tolerance for the views of others. Take a look at the discussion idea on **page 138** in **Chapter 7**.

- Use the "Turn and Teach" strategy explained on **page 138** in **Chapter 7**.

> Set up a classroom community where duties and responsibilities are shared.

> Involve students in decision-making.

Positively Contagious!

Positive affirmations are a powerful classroom tool that foster enthusiasm, promote self-esteem, and set the tone for an atmosphere conducive to learning. Model positive affirmations for your students by verbalizing positive expectations and giving yourself verbal pats-on-the-back. For example, after reading a story aloud, say, "I like the way I read that story." Or after teaching a mini-lesson, say, "I did a good job explaining that." When you model positive affirmations, students feel comfortable making positive comments about themselves and their work.

Set a positive tone for your classroom community.

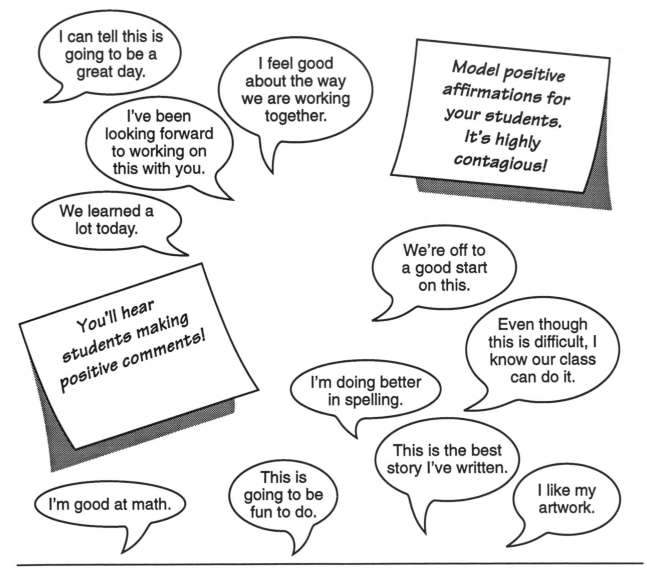

REMEMBER—an educational expert with terrific ideas for your classroom can be found by looking in a mirror! You have the best knowledge about your classroom, your students, and the way you teach most effectively.

NOTES

NOTES

The Rationale

Reading aloud is an important learning activity with a wealth of benefits for all students because it

- models the reading process positively
- exposes students to rich vocabulary
- provides students with new information
- exposes students to books that are above their independent reading levels
- introduces students to different genres
- provides a pleasurable listening activity
- gives students an opportunity to listen and use their imaginative abilities
- helps you share the joy of literature

Reading aloud offers many benefits.

Mystery Sentences

Mystery-sentence cards provide an enjoyable, high-interest literature activity. Whenever you read aloud, make a mystery-sentence card. Jot the title and author of the book on a card. When you finish reading the book or a chapter of the book aloud, take a moment to copy a sentence or two from the text onto the card. (Dialog works especially well.) Eventually you will have a set of cards containing sentences from a variety of books. Read the sentences from one of the cards aloud. Ask students to name the book, the author, and the characters who are speaking.

Make sure that books read are not forgotten.

Mystery-Sentence Card

"Don't be too sure of getting the prize, son," Father said. "It isn't size that counts as much as quality."

front

Farmer Boy
by Laura Ingalls Wilder

back

Read-Aloud Book Box

After reading a book aloud, place it in a special box. Students enjoy reading books they have heard you read aloud.

Talking Books

Talking books are books accompanied by audio tapes. You can create a set of talking books for your classroom during class time. Choose 10 books from your classroom library that can be read aloud in 10 to 15 minutes. Buy 10 inexpensive blank audio tapes. Number the books and the tapes from 1 to 10 and place each book and cassette in a zip-lock plastic bag. Record yourself as you read each book aloud to your class. When all the books have been recorded, place them in a special box. Students will enjoy hearing you read their favorite stories to them again either in the classroom or at home through a talking-book check-out system.

There are many ways to extend the excitement generated by books you read aloud.

A Special Gift

Generate excitement about the books you plan to read aloud to your class. At the beginning of the year, gift-wrap the books and place them in a basket. When you are ready to read a book aloud, have a student choose one from the basket and unwrap the surprise.

Publishing a Commemorative Book

After reading a book aloud that your students especially enjoyed, help them make a commemorative book about the story. This activity links reading, writing, talking, and listening.

Steps for Making a Commemorative Book

1. Read the book aloud. Discuss the story.

2. Ask students to dictate sentences about important events in the story. As they do, write each sentence on a 12" x 18" piece of paper. Elicit enough sentences so you have one page for every two students.

3. Give each page to a pair of students. Have them illustrate the sentence on the page.

Make reading an event to commemorate.

Classroom publishing is a great way to increase your classroom library.

Ira couldn't sleep without Tah Tah.

Ira's big sister liked to tease him.

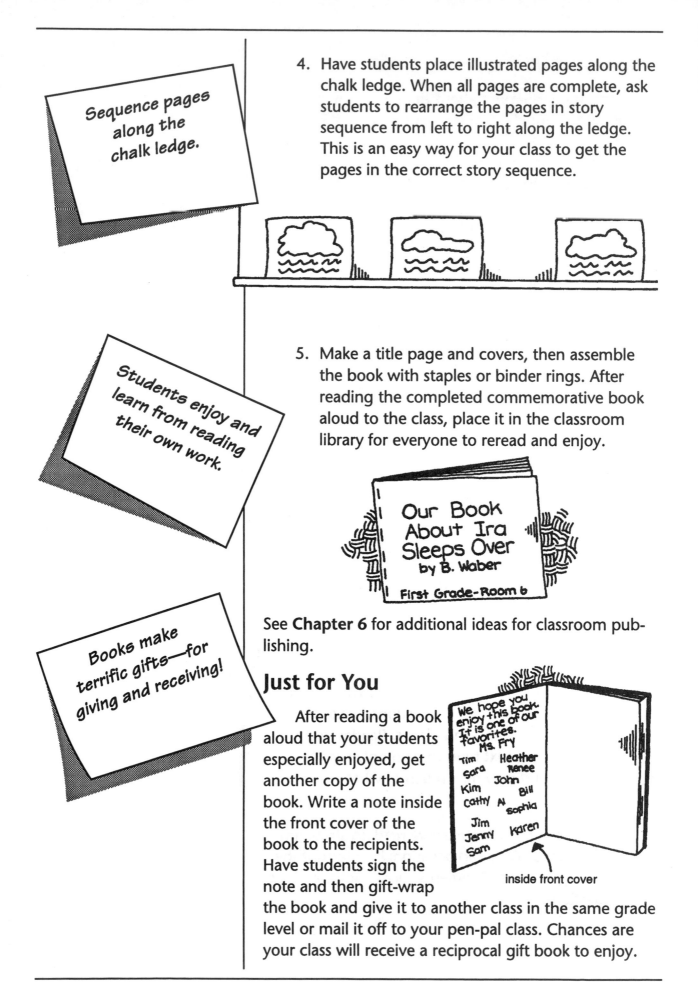

> Sequence pages along the chalk ledge.

4. Have students place illustrated pages along the chalk ledge. When all pages are complete, ask students to rearrange the pages in story sequence from left to right along the ledge. This is an easy way for your class to get the pages in the correct story sequence.

> Students enjoy and learn from reading their own work.

5. Make a title page and covers, then assemble the book with staples or binder rings. After reading the completed commemorative book aloud to the class, place it in the classroom library for everyone to reread and enjoy.

Our Book About Ira Sleeps Over
by B. Waber

First Grade-Room 6

See **Chapter 6** for additional ideas for classroom publishing.

Just for You

> Books make terrific gifts—for giving and receiving!

After reading a book aloud that your students especially enjoyed, get another copy of the book. Write a note inside the front cover of the book to the recipients. Have students sign the note and then gift-wrap

We hope you enjoy this book. It is one of our favorites.
Ms. Fry

Tim   Heather
Sara   Renee
Kim   John
Cathy Al   Bill
         Sophia
Jim
Jenny   Karen
Sam

inside front cover

the book and give it to another class in the same grade level or mail it off to your pen-pal class. Chances are your class will receive a reciprocal gift book to enjoy.

Understanding Story Structure

Help students develop a sense of story through discussions. After reading aloud, ask students questions.

- What was the problem or situation in the story?
- How did the characters attempt to solve the problem?
- How was the problem solved?
- How did the characters react or feel at the end of the story?

Help students develop a sense of story.

Special Book Display

Ask staff members about their favorite children's books. Set up a display showing a favorite book of the principal, librarian, and other staff members. Label each book with staff members' names. Invite various staff members to read their favorite books aloud to your class or to tell your students why those books are their favorites.

Model Interactive Reading

Skillful readers interact with the text. They internalize information and silently ask questions, make predictions, and visualize people and places. Readers who do not interact with the text tend to gain only surface comprehension and may miss much of what reading has to offer.

Let children see that adults enjoy and value books.

Teachers can model interactive reading strategies as they read aloud. They can occasionally interrupt their oral reading by making comments, predictions, and by asking questions.

Using Journals With Read-Aloud Books

Look for ways to link reading and writing throughout the learning day.

Grades K-1

Staple large pieces of chart paper to make a giant journal. After reading a book aloud, have students dictate sentences about the beginning, middle, and end of the story. Write the date, book title, author, and sentences elicited from students in the class journal. Read the entry aloud and then have students reread the sentences aloud together. Continue to add entries about other books you read to the class. As you write in the class journal, you are modeling the journal-writing process.

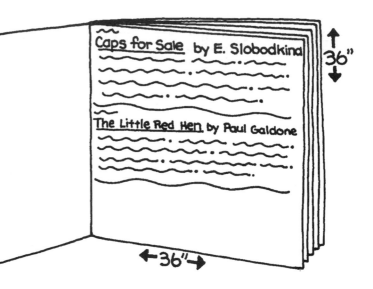

Grades 2-6

Have students make a special journal to go with a chapter book you are going to read aloud. After reading the first chapter aloud, elicit a few sentences about the chapter to write on the chalkboard. Then have students write a sentence or two in their individual journals about the chapter. Students can refer to the sentences on the chalkboard for ideas. As you write the sentences on the chalkboard, you are modeling the writing activity.

When you have finished reading the book aloud, students will have an entry about each chapter. They can then make a title page, write a critique of the book, and illustrate the covers for the journal.

Reading Nursery Rhymes and Folklore

Many of today's students are unfamiliar with traditional nursery rhymes and folklore. Fill in the gap in your students' literacy by reading these classic rhymes and stories aloud. Read nursery rhymes aloud to K-1 students. Encourage students to memorize nursery rhymes. Read folklore aloud to all students.

Creating Books About Books

Chapter Books

When you read aloud books with chapters, have students create a book about the book. After hearing each chapter, have students draw a picture and write a sentence about it. At the end of the book, students will have a page with an illustration and sentence about each chapter. Let them then compile pages into a book adding a title page and covers.

Making books about books offers children a way to respond to the literature they hear.

Making books is fun and easy!

Storybooks

On three pieces of art paper have students draw pictures about the beginning, middle, and end of a story. Instruct students to write a sentence on each page. Have students then make a title page and covers and compile the pages into a story about the book.

The Three Bears

Amy B.

Front Cover

12" x 18"

My Book About The Three Bears

Title Page

Goldilocks went for a walk in the woods.

Beginning

The three bears came home.

Middle

...ocks got scared ran back home.

End

The End

Back Cover

READING ALOUD AT HOME—Inform students' families of the joys and benefits of reading aloud at home. Reproduce the sign-and-send letters on pages 27 and 28 for students to take home at different times during the school year and encourage parents to share the joy of literature by reading aloud with their children.

Date_____

Dear Families,

One of the most enjoyable and important times of the school day is when I read aloud to the children. Students of all ages enjoy listening to stories. Reading aloud benefits students in so many ways.

- It gives students an opportunity to use their imaginations as they listen and visualize the story.

- Students are often inspired to read other books by the same author.

- Students are exposed to a wide range of literature.

- Students can enjoy hearing stories that might be too difficult for them to read independently. Students expand their understanding of new vocabulary words through listening to stories.

- Reading aloud to children can foster a life-long love for reading.

If there are younger children in your family, perhaps your school-age child can read aloud to younger family members.

At school, students look forward to our read-aloud time. Perhaps you can establish a regular time at home to read aloud with your child. You and your child will benefit from reading together!

_____

Teacher

FS-8128 *100% Practical*

Date_____

Dear Families,

    These book titles are favorites of students in our class. If you visit the library, perhaps you can help your child find these popular books. You might also want to consider these titles if you are buying books for your child.

_____

_____

_____

_____

_____

_____

_____

_____

Teacher

FS-8128 *100% Practical*

NOTES

29

NOTES

> Shared reading is perfect for grades K–6.

Definition

In shared reading the teacher and students read aloud together. Shared reading, conducted as a whole-class activity, is a wonderful way to start the learning day in K–6 classrooms.

Benefits of Shared Reading

Shared reading is an enjoyable experience in which everyone participates. It is a valuable language activity for all students in kindergarten through sixth grade. Shared reading benefits students in many ways:

- Students enjoy hearing the teacher read a poem aloud.
- The shared-reading experience provides a model for reading from left to right and understanding print for beginning readers.
- Students reading aloud with others can read with smoothness and expression.
- Shared reading places meaning before analysis.
- It affords an opportunity to teach skills in context.

> Your basal reader contains lots of poems for shared reading.

Shared-Reading Materials

Poems, chants, and song lyrics can be printed on the chalkboard, printed on charts, or reproduced so each student has a copy. Big Books can also be an excellent source of material for shared reading with primary students.

In addition to using charts or the chalkboard, you can use poems found in basal readers. Simply have students follow along in their books as you read the poem aloud. Discuss the poem and reread it together. In primary classrooms, shared-reading poems are often presented on charts. In intermediate classrooms, poems in basal readers are highly effective for shared-reading activities.

Nursery Rhymes and Songs for Shared Reading

Reproducible nursery rhymes and poems are provided on **pages 33–42**. After using the nursery rhymes for shared-reading activities, staple them into booklets for students to take home.

Use nursery rhymes for shared reading in K–1 classes.

I'll read these to my Grandma.

My Book of Nursery Rhymes

Lyn

Read, discuss, reread.

Shared Reading—Easy As 1, 2, 3

Step 1. *The teacher reads the poem aloud.* For K–1 classes, track the print on the chart by sweeping your fingertips under the words as you read aloud. This helps students understand that reading progresses from left to right and that print conveys meaning. If the poem is in the basal reader, tell students to look at the words in their books as you read aloud.

Step 2. *Teacher and students discuss the content and meaning of the poem.* Students have heard you read the poem aloud and they understand what it is about.

Step 3. *Teacher and students reread the poem aloud together.* Add enjoyment to shared reading by using different rereading strategies each day.

The Star-Spangled Banner

O, say! can you see,
    by the dawn's early light,

What so proudly we hailed
    at the twilight's last gleaming,

Whose broad stripes and bright stars,
    through the perilous fight,

O'er the ramparts we watched
    were so gallantly streaming?

And the rockets' red glare,
    the bombs bursting in air,

Gave proof through the night
    that our flag was still there.

O, say, does that Star-Spangled
    Banner yet wave

O'er the land of the free
    and home of the brave?

— Francis Scott Key

FS-8128 *100% Practical*

America
(My Country 'Tis of Thee)

My country, 'tis of thee,
Sweet land of liberty,
Of thee I sing;

Land where my fathers died!
Land of the Pilgrims' pride!
From ev'ry mountainside,
Let freedom ring!

—Samuel Francis Smith
1831

reproducible page

The Itsy, Bitsy Spider

The itsy, bitsy spider
Climbed up the waterspout.

Down came the rain
And washed the spider out.

Out came the sun
And dried up all the rain.

And the itsy, bitsy spider
Climbed up the spout again.

FS-8128 *100% Practical*

The ABC Song

A, B, C, D, E, F, G,
H, I, J, K, L-M-N-O-P,
Q, R, S, and T, U, V,
W, X, and Y, and Z.
Now I know my A, B, C's,
Next time won't you sing with me?

reproducible page

FS-8128 *100% Practical*

Twinkle, Twinkle, Little Star

Twinkle, twinkle, little star,
How I wonder what you are!
Up above the world so high,
Like a diamond in the sky,
Twinkle, twinkle, little star,
How I wonder what you are!

reproducible page

© Frank Schaffer Publications, Inc. FS-8128 *100% Practical*

One, Two, Buckle My Shoe

One, two,
Buckle my shoe.

Three, four,
Shut the door.

Five, six,
Pick up sticks.

Seven, eight,
Lay them straight.

Nine, ten,
A big fat hen.

FS-8128 *100% Practical*

Humpty Dumpty

Humpty Dumpty sat on a wall,
Humpty Dumpty had a great fall;
All the King's horses and all the King's men
Couldn't put Humpty together again.

FS-8128 *100% Practical*

The Cat and the Fiddle

Hey, diddle, diddle, the cat and the fiddle,
The cow jumped over the moon;
The little dog laughed to see such sport,
And the dish ran away with the spoon.

Jack and Jill

Jack and Jill went up the hill
To fetch a pail of water.
Jack fell down and broke his crown,
And Jill came tumbling after.

reproducible page

FS-8128 *100% Practical*

Thirty Days Hath September

Thirty days hath September,
April, June, and November;
All the rest have thirty-one,
Except February alone,
Which has twenty-eight days clear
And twenty-nine in each leap year.

reproducible page

Rereading Strategies

- **Choral Reading**—Have the entire class reread aloud together.

- **Echo Me Reading**—After the teacher reads a line of the poem aloud, the class reads it aloud, echoing the teacher. This helps students read expressively, as they tend to imitate the expression modeled by the teacher.

- **Taking Turns**— Call on a student or pairs of students to read aloud a line of the poem. Then have the whole class read the next line aloud.

- **Group Reading**—Divide the class into groups. Have groups take turns reading lines or verses aloud together.

- **Shared-Reading Partners**—List students' names in pairs on the chalkboard. Reread the shared-reading poem aloud with the entire class. At some time during the school day shared-reading partners reread the poem aloud together. When they do this they check off their names on the chalkboard.

Look in the library for a book of jump-rope rhymes. Many of these are perfect for shared reading.

Teaching Skills With Shared Reading

Read and enjoy the poem with your class by following the three steps for shared reading:

1. Teacher reads aloud.
2. Teacher and students discuss the meaning.
3. Teacher and students reread aloud together.

Once students have read, understood, and enjoyed the whole selection, do a focus lesson that complements the material you are using. After teaching a focus lesson, give students an opportunity to practice and apply what they have learned. Here is a sample focus lesson linked to shared reading.

Shared-Reading Skills Lesson

1. The teacher displays a poem on a chart or the chalkboard. The teacher reads the poem aloud, tracking the print from left to right.

2. The teacher elicits comments from the class about the poem. They discuss the content, interpretation, and whatever was interesting and/or enjoyable about the selection.

3. The class rereads the poem aloud.

4. The teacher identifies a skill or concept that can be taught through the shared-reading selection. (Ideas follow.)

5. Following skill presentation, give students opportunities to practice and apply the skills and concepts from focus lessons. This can be achieved by such varied activities as these:

- rereading the poem aloud

- using a worksheet to reinforce the concept

- having students demonstrate the skill through class reading and writing activities

Teach skills in context through shared reading.

Identify a skill that could be introduced from the text of the selection.

Perfect for short *i* practice.

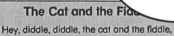

The Cat and the Fiddle

Hey, diddle, diddle, the cat and the fiddle,
The cow jumped over the moon;
The little dog laughed to see such sport,
And the dish ran away with the spoon.

Ideas!

- If you are using a poem on a chart, clip a piece of clear plastic over the chart. Now you can write on the plastic overlay without actually marking on the chart.

Fasten charts together with binder rings to make a big book.

Help me find the number words. I'll underline them.

- Give students a copy of the poem. To maximize participation, have students do activities right on their copies of the poem.

Let's look for words that rhyme.

Laminate charts so they last "forever"!

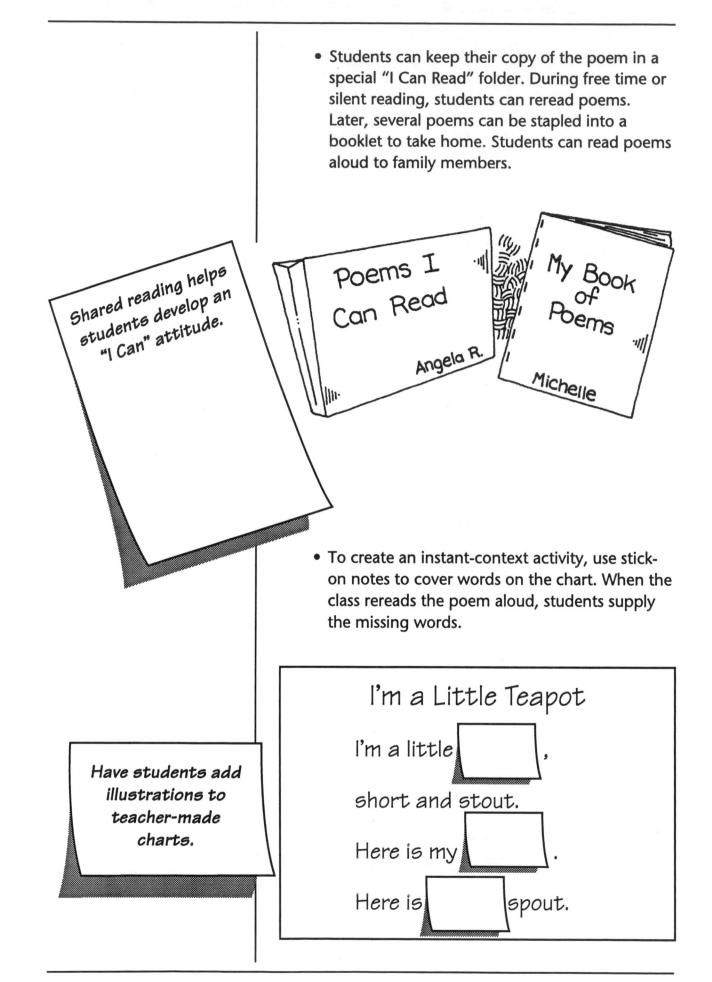

• Students can keep their copy of the poem in a special "I Can Read" folder. During free time or silent reading, students can reread poems. Later, several poems can be stapled into a booklet to take home. Students can read poems aloud to family members.

Shared reading helps students develop an "I Can" attitude.

Poems I Can Read

Angela R.

My Book of Poems

Michelle

• To create an instant-context activity, use stick-on notes to cover words on the chart. When the class rereads the poem aloud, students supply the missing words.

Have students add illustrations to teacher-made charts.

I'm a Little Teapot

I'm a little ____,

short and stout.

Here is my ____.

Here is ____ spout.

- You can use stick-on notes to cover initial or final consonants, plurals, and/or affixes. Challenge students to identify what's hidden.

Charts are a wonderful, reusable source for shared reading. Take a look at the ideas on **page 250** in **Chapter 13** for storing and organizing charts in your classroom!

Tell me the missing letter.

Follow up shared reading with skills reinforcement.

Let's look for words that rhyme.

Provide shared-reading activities daily for your students.

NOTES

Variety—The Spice of Reading

A balanced reading program includes a variety of reading materials and ways of grouping students. Grouping practices can include whole class, small groups, pairs of students, and individual students. Students benefit from opportunities to work and learn in different kinds of groups.

Expose students to a variety of books.

Reading Materials

Literature-based reading instruction, in my view, can take place in the context of trade books (works of literature) and/or textbooks (literature-based basals). How the material is actually used is more critical than if the story is in a trade book or textbook. Follow these general guidelines:

- Teach skills in meaningful contexts.

- Link reading, writing, speaking, and listening.

- Use reading material at students' instructional levels.

Literature links reading, writing, speaking, and listening.

Kinds of Books

Books are available in a variety of levels and types. Some contain mostly illustrations, some mostly words, and others a mix of illustrations and words. Some books follow patterns, such as those that repeat the same refrain throughout the book. In cumulative books, one item is added to a list or refrain each time it is repeated.

Coordinating Literature Across Grade Levels

Many schools designate specific works of literature for certain grade levels within schools or throughout school districts. Why? If a fourth-grade teacher reads *James and the Giant Peach* aloud to her class and the following year the fifth-grade teacher plans to use the same book in his reading program, many of his students will already know the story.

When students already know the story, teachers cannot use prediction activities connected with reading. Therefore, it makes sense for teachers to coordinate lists of literature and designate certain titles as reading books for students and others as read-aloud books for the grade level. Over time the book lists for grade levels can be adjusted and new books can be added, but a school-wide agreement can help a literature program run smoothly and effectively.

> Establish a literature plan for your school.

How to Get Your Hands on More Books

Teachers and students can work together to make the classroom a gold mine of reading resources. Acquire more reading materials for your class through these strategies:

1. Birthday Books

Ask families to donate a book to the classroom library to commemorate children's birthdays instead of sending treats to school. Place a commemorative book plate inside the front covers of birthday books. Reproducible book plates are provided on **page 53**.

> *The more books you can have on hand for students, the better.*

2. Donated Books

After students buy and read books from book clubs they often toss them aside. Ask students if they have any books at home that they would like to donate to the classroom library. Tell them to ask for permission at home before donating books. Glue book plates inside front covers of donated books.

3. Magazines

Ask friends, neighbors, relatives, and school families if they have magazines they can donate to your classroom library. Magazines like *National Geographic, Cat Fancy,* and publications for children can be enjoyed by your students. Request book and magazine donations in newsletters that go out to school families.

4. Instant Storybooks

Classroom sets of outdated basal readers are stored unused in most schools, and teachers can make hundreds of storybooks from these texts. Locate outdated basals and take several copies from each grade level. Tear the books apart story by story, add oak-tag covers and staple them to create storybooks. Place the books in a box or basket in your classroom. As students read the books, they can write story titles and illustrate the covers.

The books are free, students enjoy them, and they provide reading-practice opportunities. When parents ask for sources of reading practice at home, teachers can offer students these books. Round up some of those old basals and you can easily create hundreds of storybooks at a variety of reading levels.

There are lots of creative ways to increase your classroom library.

Make books recycling old basals.

Jim's New Puppy

cover by Bill M.

5. Hidden Treasury

Enlist students and their families in this fund-raising idea that can generate dollars for books. Raise funds to buy books through recycling aluminum cans for cash. Ask a parent to take charge of this fund-raising effort.

Buy a large trash can and plastic trash-can liners. Have students bring aluminum cans to school. Make your parent-helper responsible for collecting the cans from your classroom every few weeks, taking them to a "cash for cans" recycling center, and giving the money to you at school.

If you like, first reimburse yourself for the purchase of the trash can and liners, then set aside the rest of the money in a special fund. Purchase books for your classroom with this money. You will be amazed at how much money you can generate when students gather cans from neighbors and relatives.

Teachers can place a container for cans in the teachers' room and gather cans at meetings and seminars. This cooperative effort to raise funds for books builds classroom team spirit and enhances your classroom library.

Keep track of your book fund on the chalkboard so students know the results of their efforts.

Raise classroom team spirit as you raise cash for books.

chalkboard	
Class Treasury	
8.55	Nov. 11
−7.00	cost of big can
1.55	balance
+6.75	Dec. 15
8.30	balance
+10.20	Jan. 22
18.50	balance
−12.55	book order
5.95	balance

This book is

for _____

from _____

This book
is from

_____

_____

For

_____

From

_____

This book is
especially for

_____

from

_____

reproducible page

53

FS-8128 *100% Practical*

Grouping for Instruction

Your reading program should include whole-class, small-group, pairs of students, and individual activities. Every class contains students with a range of reading and writing skills from weak to strong. Through varied grouping practices you can address the instructional needs of all students.

I recommend starting the year with whole-class reading. Keeping everyone together for the first few weeks of school:

- fosters team spirit

- helps bond the class

- is non-threatening to students

- gives you an opportunity to get to know the class

After getting to know students' reading and writing abilities, teachers can perform some flexible grouping, which is described below.

Whole-class shared reading activities can be done every day throughout the school year. Occasionally, the whole class be treated as one big group and can read together for a few weeks, and then flexible grouping can be resumed.

Whole-Class Reading

1. Shared reading poems and chants are wonderful whole-class reading activities. Take a look at **Chapter 3** for ways to make the most of shared reading in your classroom.

2. Have your class read a work of literature using a classroom set of books. Choose a book that is readable for most of your students. It will be too difficult for some students and too easy for others. Use prereading, reading, and postreading activities in this chapter with basals or trade books.

A balanced program includes large-group, small-group and individual activities.

Shared reading is an enjoyable whole-class activity.

Flexible Grouping

The purpose of grouping, in my view, is to better meet the instructional needs of students in the group. With flexible grouping, your most capable students are reading challenging material and the weakest readers are using material that is appropriate for them. You can focus on skills students need and teach those skills in context. Flexible grouping throughout the year is dynamic, not static. Group membership does not remain constant throughout the year; students are grouped according to their needs.

Partner Reading

Assign students to a reading partner for the month. Reading partners can do these activities:

- take turns reading pages orally

- read silently together, then discuss the selection

- sit facing opposite directions as shown above

Groups should be dynamic, not static.

Cooperative learning works!

Individual Reading Activities

Sustained Silent Reading—Occasionally ask a few students to share something about the books they are reading for silent reading. This gives students an opportunity to spread the word about the books they enjoy.

Enrichment Reading—Set up an enrichment reading center in your classroom as shown on **page 181** in **Chapter 9**.

Prereading, Reading, and Postreading Activities

Students' reading experiences are enriched by providing activities that prepare them for reading and by appropriate follow-up. There are many ways to provide reading activities before students read, as they read, and after reading.

A variety of suggested activities appears on the following pages.

Prereading Activities

1. Making Predictions

Read the title aloud. Introduce the characters by telling their names and a few words about them. Then ask students to make predictions about the story.

2. Making Predictions, Creating Interest

Before reading a book from beginning to end, read aloud a few pages from the book. If the book has 100 pages, have students call out three page numbers between 1 and 100. Read those three pages aloud and then ask the class to predict what the story might be like. This piques curiosity and interest in the book. If the book is a storybook with unnumbered pages, simply flip the book open and read a page at random aloud.

Lead students into, through, and beyond books.

Pique students' interest with prereading activities.

Reading (as you read) Activities

1. Oral Language, Sequencing

Stop part way through the story and ask students to summarize the story up that point. Ask the group "How did the story start?" After a student responds, ask "What happened next?" Continue to lead students through an oral summary up to the stopping point. Then encourage the class to predict what will happen next.

Enrich reading by relating the characters to students' own lives or experiences.

2. Oral Language, Writing

Have students react to characters in their journals or in a discussion. Ideas for questions about characters include

- Have you ever felt the way the main character feels?

- Is there a character you would like to have for a friend? Why or why not?

- Would you like to be the main character? Why or why not?

- What question would you ask the character?

- If these characters were speaking from behind a curtain so that you couldn't see them, would you be able to tell who was speaking by the words he or she said? Why or why not?

- Which character is most like you? Which is least like you? Why?

- How does the setting (time and place of the story) affect how the characters act?

- What do you like best and least about the main character(s)?

3. Understanding Literature

If the class or a group is bogged down reading through a chapter book, provide a boost by reading a chapter aloud. Have students follow along as you read.

4. Enjoying Literature, Understanding Dialog

After reading a story or chapter, have a group of students practice reading parts aloud from a scene in the chapter. Assign students to take the parts of different characters in the scene and one to be the narrator. Have the rest of the class follow along in their books. This helps students understand dialog and the use of quotation marks.

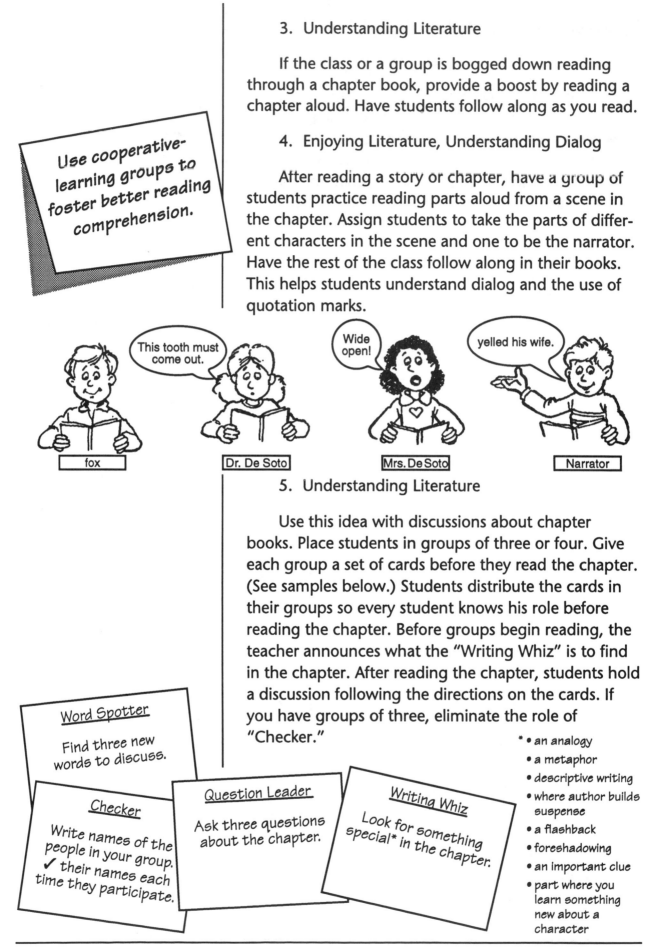

> Use cooperative-learning groups to foster better reading comprehension.

This tooth must come out. — fox

Dr. De Soto

Wide open! — Mrs. De Soto

yelled his wife. — Narrator

5. Understanding Literature

Use this idea with discussions about chapter books. Place students in groups of three or four. Give each group a set of cards before they read the chapter. (See samples below.) Students distribute the cards in their groups so every student knows his role before reading the chapter. Before groups begin reading, the teacher announces what the "Writing Whiz" is to find in the chapter. After reading the chapter, students hold a discussion following the directions on the cards. If you have groups of three, eliminate the role of "Checker."

Word Spotter

Find three new words to discuss.

Checker

Write names of the people in your group. ✓ their names each time they participate.

Question Leader

Ask three questions about the chapter.

Writing Whiz

Look for something special* in the chapter.

* • an analogy
• a metaphor
• descriptive writing
• where author builds suspense
• a flashback
• foreshadowing
• an important clue
• part where you learn something new about a character

Postreading Activities

1. Oral Language, Sequencing

Retelling can be done after reading a chapter or an entire book, with a small group or the whole class. Ask students to describe how the story started, what happened next, and so on. Continue talking students through the story in sequence until you have asked students to tell how the story ended.

2. Oral Language, Sequencing, Writing

Create a chart story or written summary about the story. As your students retell the story as described above, write sentences elicited from the class on a chart.

> Postreading activities extend appreciation of literature.

Imogene's Antlers

Imogene lived in a big house.
She had her own bedroom.
Imogene has no brothers or sisters.

3. Sequencing, Summarizing, Writing

Have students write a three-sentence summary in their journals. Students write a sentence about the beginning, middle, and end of the story.

4. Creative Expression

Have students discuss or write a different ending for the story. Students can do this individually, with a partner, or in small groups. Teachers can elicit ideas from the class and write them on the chalkboard.

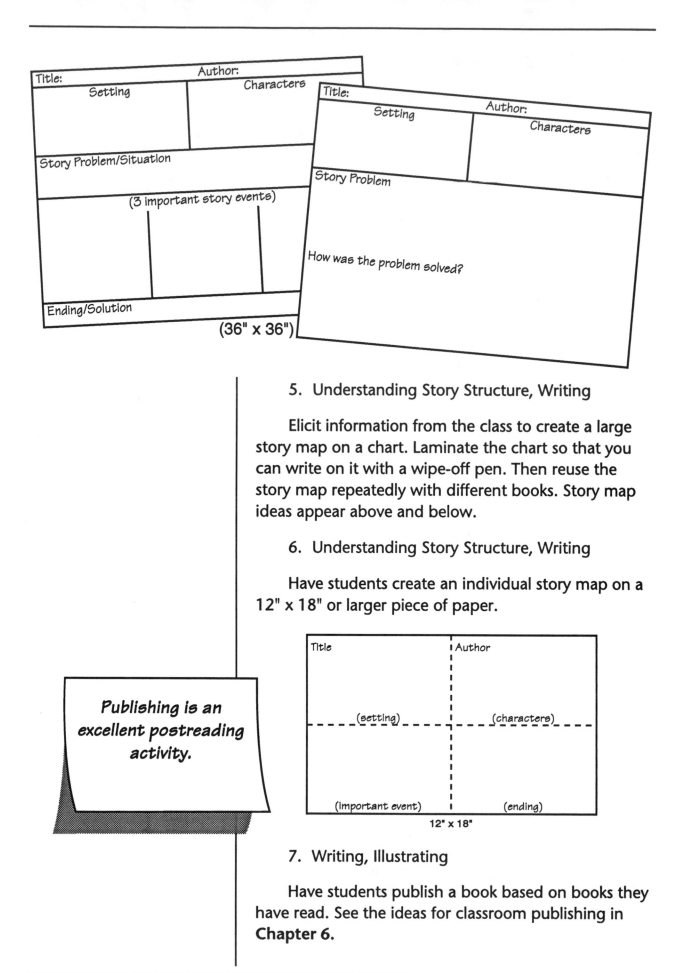

5. Understanding Story Structure, Writing

Elicit information from the class to create a large story map on a chart. Laminate the chart so that you can write on it with a wipe-off pen. Then reuse the story map repeatedly with different books. Story map ideas appear above and below.

6. Understanding Story Structure, Writing

Have students create an individual story map on a 12" x 18" or larger piece of paper.

Publishing is an excellent postreading activity.

7. Writing, Illustrating

Have students publish a book based on books they have read. See the ideas for classroom publishing in **Chapter 6**.

8. Enjoying Literature, Oral Language

Tear a paperback book into chapters and staple chapters into booklets. Give each chapter to a different student to read. After individual students have read their chapters, have those students present a book review for the class. Announce the book's title and author. Then have the student who read chapter one tell about the chapter, followed by the student who read chapter two. Continue to do this for all the chapters in sequence. Place all chapters in a zip-lock bag labeled with the book's title and author. Place it in your classroom library.

9. Oral Language, Evaluating Literature

After reading a story, divide students into groups of three or four. Have students sit in a circle and informally chat about the book.

10. Phonics, Structural Analysis

Have students do word hunts using the book or chapter they just read. Have students skim back through the story for words to use in their word hunts.

Use a variey of postreading activities to keep interest alive.

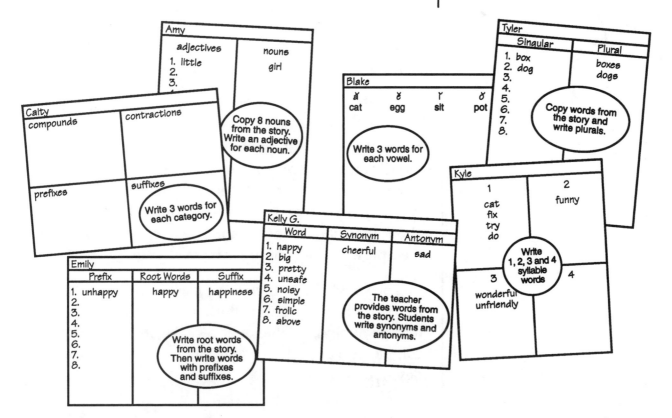

Word hunts can be done as small-group or whole-class activities. Simply write the word-hunt categories on the chalkboard. Then ask students to skim back through the story they read to find words that fit the categories. Students call out the words for the teacher to write on the chalkboard.

chalkboard

plurals	compounds	contractions
boxes		don't
dogs		

backpack

Postreading activities can be done following entire books or chapter by chapter.

11. Understanding Literature, Sequencing

Wrap up reading with a book review. This activity works with both chapter books and storybooks:

For Chapter Books—Divide your class into groups, creating the same number of groups as there are chapters in the book. Assign each group to a different chapter. Give groups time to prepare a project and/or presentation about their assigned chapter. For example, you might have groups choose to make a large mural about the chapter or to dramatize it. Have groups give their presentations for the class in chapter order.

For Storybooks—Divide the class into five groups. Assign each group one of these topics: setting, characters, beginning, middle or end of the story. Each group completes a project or presentation about their topic as described above.

12. Understanding Characters

Have students trace their hand prints and write the name of a story character on the outline. Students write a character trait on each finger.

13. Understanding Literature

Create charts about characters to help students understand the characters and relate literature to their own lives. Elicit information from students to record on a large chart. Or, have individual students make character charts on 12" x 18" pieces of paper. Take a look at the ideas that follow for charts that focus on characters.

Chapter 11, "Learning Activities and Projects," is filled with more ideas to enhance reading and literature.

A Character Study

The book title is _____. The author is _____.

Who?	Did What?	When?	Where?	Why?

Character Charts

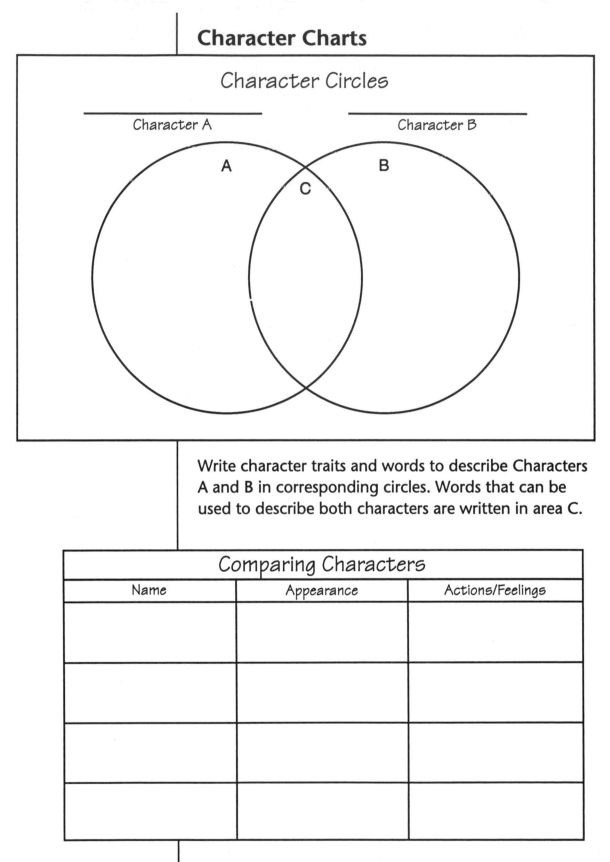

Character Circles

Character A   Character B

A   C   B

Write character traits and words to describe Characters A and B in corresponding circles. Words that can be used to describe both characters are written in area C.

Comparing Characters

Name	Appearance	Actions/Feelings

14. Chapter 11

Learning Activites and Projects is filled with ideas to enhance reading and literature.

Special Approaches to Literature

When teachers use several books that are related by theme, they have opportunities to use literature in more powerful ways. The common element, or connection, can be author, illustrator, or theme/topic. Special approaches such as genre study and textsets foster critical thinking, enhance the process of seeing relationships, and foster recognition of connections between literature and ourselves.

Genre study and textsets can be used at all grade levels with books students read themselves or ones the teacher reads aloud. Your students can contrast and compare several books by the same author or illustrator. Ways to use both genre study and textsets follow.

Genre Study

1. Divide your class into groups and have each group gather and display books in a specific genre:

Picture Books	Poetry
Science	Folklore
Historical Fiction	Fantasy
Informational Books	Biography

2. Consider focusing on a different genre each month of the school year. By the end of the school year, a class of students can complete 10 genre studies.

3. Post a list of books in the genre that your students would enjoy reading. Or, use reproducible form on the following page to give students copies of prepared lists. These can come from district core-literature lists, suggested readings from social studies or science materials, or a tailor-made compilation of your own or your students' favorites. Your school librarian may also have book lists by grade level or topic.

Genre study adds interest to literature.

Expose students to a variety of genres.

_____ **Books**

Genre

For You to Read

_____

_____

_____

_____

_____

_____

_____

_____

_____

_____

_____

Teacher Note: Reproduce this page, write in the genre and list books your students would enjoy.

reproducible page

Textsets

Textsets are two or more books that are related in some way. Books can be related by having the same illustrator, author, theme or topic. I recommend using books that are connected by topic or theme. Using related books is a powerful way of using literature for all grade levels. Here are some ways to use textsets:

1. Choose two books that have the same theme. For example, books with the theme of friendship. Read aloud, or have students read, one book about friendship. Discuss the setting, characters, and plot. Students can write in their journals about the book or you can elicit information to write on a story map (**see page 60**), character chart (**see pages 63–64**), or a chart that compares books (**see pages 69–70**). Then read, discuss, and add information to the chart about the other book in the text set. After having read and discussed the books separately, hold a discussion to analyze, contrast, and compare the textset by discussing these points:

- How are the characters are alike and different?

- How are the friendships are alike and different?

- How do the story situation/problems differ?

- How do the characters and friendships in the books relate to students' personal experiences?

Recording information about the textset on a chart or the chalkboard helps students organize information and see relationships.

2. "My First Choice" gives students a chance to choose the book they want to read in the textset. Choose a textset of three or four books that have the same theme. You will need six or eight copies of each book. Show your class the books and tell them a little bit about each one. Then have students indicate on paper the books that are their first and second choices to read. Group students according to their choices.

Textsets are books that are related by author, illustrator, theme, or topic.

Textsets foster critical thinking.

Making decisions empowers students.

You will not be able to give every student his or her first choice. Tell students you will keep track of this and, at another time when choices are offered, those students who do not get their first choice this time will get it next time.

Group students according to their choices and have groups read their books. Then compare and contrast the books through discussions and post-reading activities such as story maps **(page 60)**, character charts **(pages 63–64)**, or book comparison charts **(pages 69–70)**.

A grid will enhance discussions about textsets.

3. Enhance textsets by choosing a book to read aloud to your class that falls into the textset of books that students are reading. Then when you discuss the text set you can include the read-aloud book to enrich the discussion.

4. Textset Grid. On a bulletin board or large chart, make a grid that goes with your textset. The grid is a visual representation of the textset and helps students see similarities, differences, and connections between the books.

For example, let's say your class is reading three different books that have a theme of survival, and you are also reading a book aloud with a survival theme. As books are discussed, write information on the Textset Grid about each book.

If groups are reading different books, each section can be responsible for completing information about its book on the grid. The teacher can complete information about the book she is reading aloud. Look on **pages 69–70** for an example of a Textset Grid and examples of book-comparison charts that can be used with textsets.

Textsets and Book Comparisons

Textset Theme				
Titles				
Setting				
Characters				
Story Situation or Problem				
Attempts to solve problem				
How the problem was solved				
How characters felt at the end of the story				

Comparing Books

The theme is _____.

Title		
Setting		
Main Characters		
Problem		
Attempts to solve the problem		
How the problem was solved		
How characters felt at the end		

Why not trade books with another class? Their "used" books will be "new" to you!

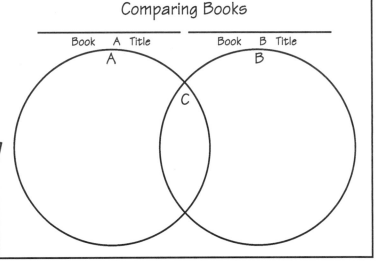

Comparing Books

Book A Title _____ Book B Title _____

Information about books A and B is written in corresponding circles. Information that pertains to both books is written in Area C.

Start a Classroom Book Exchange

Make the most of books students buy from book clubs. Place six or eight paperback books from the classroom library in the book-exchange box or basket. Tell students they can take a book from the box in exchange for one of the books that they are ready to give away. Books in the box will constantly change allowing students to read a variety of books. Why not start a book and magazine exchange for teachers in the teachers' room?

Time to Read

Reading is the best way to start the day—every day—all year long in the classroom. Capture lost minutes at the beginning of each day by having students read books of their choice. When students enter the room, after taking care of morning business (hanging up coats, signing up for lunch, and so on), they should read quietly until the teacher is ready to greet the class and start the day. Start this routine the first day of school and continue it all year. This is an enjoyable, peaceful way to begin each learning day.

> *Begin every day with reading.*

Fourth Grade
Room 6

We begin our day by:
• hanging up coats
• signing up for lunch
• turning in homework
• reading quietly

It Pays to Advertise

Look through your classroom library each week and pull out six or eight books to put on display. Post a sign on each book to catch students' attention. Once you get this started in your classroom, perhaps you can have groups of students take charge of putting books on display. Book holders are easy to make from wire hangers or cardboard.

> *Handy home-made holders let you put books on display.*

Book Holders

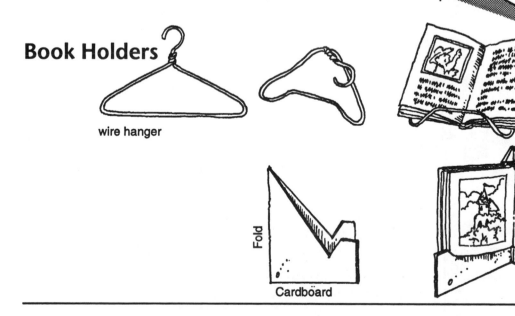

wire hanger

Fold

Cardboard

Immerse your students in literature. They will become lifelong readers and learners.

NOTES

Effective Writing Program Components

- A regularly scheduled block of time
- Opportunities for students to choose topics
- Some teacher-selected topics
- Teaching writing skills/conventions in context
- Time for some students to share their writing
- Compilation of writing portfolios

A good writing program has several important components.

Your Writing Center

Students spend several writing periods working on some writing activities; therefore, they need a place to keep their work that is in progress. Have two writing folders for each student kept in boxes or baskets at the writing center.

Organization is vital to success.

In Progress Writing Folders

Finished Work Writing Folders

Writing Folders

Give the writers in your classroom resource pages to staple into their "In Progress" writing folders. Reproducibles are provided on **pages 74–77.** Directions for making folders appear in **Chapter 8** on **page 157.**

Capitalization Rules

In Progress

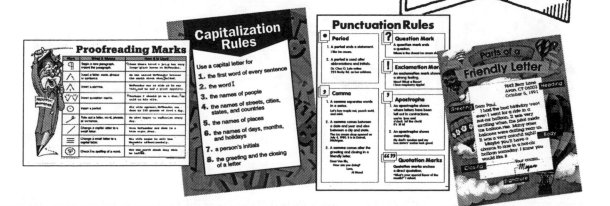

Proofreading Marks

Mark	Description	Example
¶	Begin a new paragraph. Indent the paragraph.	¶ Once there lived a jolly but very large giant known as McThunder.
∧	Insert a letter, word, phrase, or sentence.	He was called McThunder because the earth shook when ∧he walked.
∧	Insert a comma.	McThunder was as wide as he was tall ∧ and he had a giant appetite.
∨∨ ""	Insert quotation marks.	∨ Perhaps I should go on a diet, ∨ he said to his wife.
⊙	Insert a period.	His wife agreed ⊙ McThunder cut down to 140 pounds of food a day.
ℓ	Take out a letter, word, phrase, or sentence.	He also began to exerℓcise every day.
/	Change a capital letter to a small letter.	Soon McThunder was down to a trim eight /Tons.
≡	Change a small letter to a capital letter.	His wife began to call him Mcrumble affectionately. ≡
SP	Check the spelling of a word.	Now the earth shook only when he laffed. SP

FS-8128 *100% Practical*   © Frank Schaffer Publications, Inc.

Capitalization Rules

Use a capital letter for

1. the first word of every sentence

2. the word I

3. the names of people

4. the names of streets, cities, states, and countries

5. the names of places

6. the names of days, months, and holidays

7. a person's initials

8. the greeting and the closing of a letter

reproducible page

FS-8128 *100% Practical*

Punctuation Rules

● Period

1. A **period** ends a statement.

   I like ice cream.

2. A **period** is used after abbreviations and initials.

   Dr. Choc O. Late writes 224 Rocky Rd. as her address.

? Question Mark

A **question mark** ends a question.

Where is the closest ice cream shop?

! Exclamation Mark

An **exclamation mark** shows a strong feeling.

Wow! What a flavor!
I love raspberry ripple!

' Comma

1. A **comma** separates words in a series.

   Let's buy maple nut, peach swirl, and mint.

2. A **comma** comes between a date and year and also between a city and state.

   The ice cream shop opened on July 4, 1980. It is in Detroit, Michigan.

3. A **comma** comes after the greeting and closing in a friendly letter.

   Dear Van Illa,
      How are you doing?
         Love,
            Al Mond

' Apostrophe

1. An **apostrophe** shows where letters have been left out in contractions.

   you're [you are]
   o'clock [of the clock]
   it's [it is]

2. An **apostrophe** shows ownership.

   My dad's sundae and my two sisters' sodas look good.

" " Quotation Marks

Quotation marks enclose a direct quotation.

"What's your special flavor of the month?" I asked.

reproducible page

Parts of a Friendly Letter

Heading

7842 Bear Lane
Avaon, CT 06002
October 5, 1991

Greeting

Dear Paul,

    I had the best birthday treat ever! I went for a ride in a hot-air balloon. It was very exciting when the pilot made the balloon rise. Many other balloons were drifting near us. It was a very colorful sight!

    Maybe you'll have a chance to ride in a hot-air balloon someday. I know you would like it.

Body

Closing ——————— Your cousin,

Megan

Signature

FS-8128 *100% Practical*

Class Profile

Write the steps of the writing process on the chalkboard and have students use magnets with names to indicate which step they are working on as shown below. Directions appear on **page 165** in **Chapter 9**.

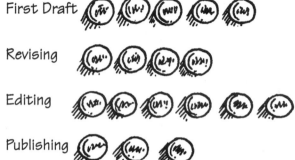

> Encourage students to take responsibility for tracking their progress.

Tracking Ticket

Have students keep track of their progress on the reproducible tracking tickets provided on the following page. Students can staple the ticket to their work in progress. Use the form on **page 79**.

> "Next-time" notes help work flow.

Helping Students With Continuity

If students must put their work aside when they are in the midst of writing, encourage them to jot a note telling what they were about to write next. Then when students continue writing on another day, their notes can help them pick up where they left off. Have the reproducible "Next Time" forms on **page 79** available for students.

Name _____ Date _____

Tracking Ticket

✓ 1. Read your writing aloud to yourself.

___ 2. Read your writing to a partner.

I read to _____.

___ 3. Revise and edit.

___ 4. Put in Teacher Conference Box. Ⓣ_____ Date _____

___ 5. Do you want to publish?

☐ Yes ☐ No   Date Publishing Done _____

Name _____

Next time I write, I'll think about

_____

_____

_____

_____

_____

Name _____

Next time I write, I'll think about

_____

_____

_____

_____

_____

reproducible page

         FS-8128 *100% Practical*

Spelling Strategies

Using inventive spellings frees students to write without stopping to get help. Using inventive spellings actually improves students' writing. Helpful spelling strategies are listed below.

1. Fostering Independence in Spelling—When students can't spell words, suggest these alternatives:

- Try writing the word until it looks right.

- Use inventive spelling.

- Ask a classmate.

- Refer to books and charts.

- Use "magic writing" to save space for the word.

"Magic writing" is a ⌇⌇⌇⌇ line used to save a space for writing a word or part of a word the student cannot spell. Students write the letters or parts of the word that they do know. Using "magic writing" allows students to continue writing without interrupting the flow of ideas. (See example below.)

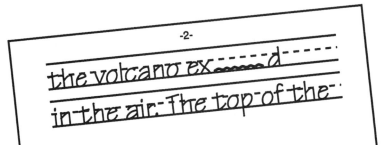

Help students become independent spellers.

- Ask students what else they can try.

- Show them where a letter is missing in the word.

- Help students find the word in books/charts.

> Insisting upon correct spelling can hamper the creative process.

> Becoming a good speller is an evolving process.

2. **The First 25**—When students do a writing activity, have them count and mark off the first 25 words. Check the first 25 words for spelling accuracy.

3. **Studying Spelling Words**—An effective method for students to use is this:

Look (Look at the word.)

Say (Say the word.)

Picture (Close your eyes and picture the word.)

Cover and write (Cover the word and write it.)

Check (Make sure you wrote it correctly.)

Give students a copy of page 82 to take home.

4. **Teaching Spelling Through Word Families**— Primary students can benefit from learning words through word families. More than 500 words can be created from the phonemes below. One way to integrate word families is to link them to shared-reading poems. For example, use a poem for shared-reading in your classroom. Use words from the poem to generate a lesson on a word family.

Teach students to use a five-step method for studying spelling words.

(chalkboard)

Jack and Jill

Jack and Jill went up the hill
To fetch a pail of water.
Jack fell down and broke his crown,
And Jill came tumbling after.

Jill
bill
hill
fill

Phonograms

_ack	_eat	_ice	_ock	_uck
_ail	_ell	_ick	_oke	_ug
_ain	_est	_ide	_op	_ug
_ake		_ight	_ore	_ump
_ale		_ill	_ot	_unk
_ame		_in		
_an		_ine		
_ank		_ing		
_ap		_ink		
_ash		_ip		
_at		_it		
_ate				
_aw				
_ay				

Step Up to Spelling Success

Use these five steps to practice words.

1. **Look** at the word.

2. **Say** the word.

friend

3. **Picture** the word.

friend

4. **Write** the word.

5. **Check** the word.

friend friend

reproducible page

5. Providing High-Frequency Words for Students—Offer easy access to high-frequency words for your students. A high-frequency word list is provided on **page 84.** You can furnish essential vocabulary words through "Pocket Dictionary" or "Wall Dictionary" bulletin boards.

Easy access to high-frequency words reduces spelling anxiety.

Pocket Dictionary Bulletin Board

Place envelopes labeled with the letters of the alphabet on a bulletin board. Write high-frequency words on index cards and file them in envelopes according to their beginning letters. Have extra index cards available. When students ask for spelling help, write words on cards for students. After students use the words, they can file them in the Pocket Dictionary on the bulletin board.

Our Pocket Dictionary

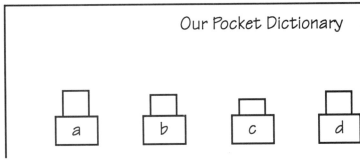

a   b   c   d

Wall Dictionary Bulletin Board/Chart

Write high-frequency words on cards. Use bold print so words are easy to see. Alphabetize the cards, then number the words. If you are using 75 words, number the bulletin board from 1 to 75. Each week, post 8 or 10 words on the wall dictionary and "test" your students on those words. Have students write the words, then check spelling tests together. As students take the test, they can refer to the wall dictionary. Eventually all the words will be posted in alphabetical order. The purpose of the "test" is simply to help students know and remember which words are posted.

Our Wall Dictionary

1.	16.	31.	46.	61.
2.	17.	32.	47. should	62.
3.	18. does	33.	48.	63.
4.	19.	34.	49.	64. until
5.	20.	35.	50.	65.
6. around	21.	36.	51.	66.
7.	22.	37.	52. stay	67.
8.	23.	38. house	53.	68.
9.	24.	39.	54.	69.
10.	25.	40.	55.	70. watch
11.	26.	41.	56. their	71.
12.	27.	42.	57.	72.
13.	28.	43.	58.	73.
14.	29.	44.	59.	74.
15. body	30.	45.	60.	75. would

Bookwords (227 words from 400 easy literature books)

a	door	just	over	then
about	down	keep	own	there
after	each	kid	papa	they
again	eat	know	pet	thing
all	ever	lady	play	think
always	every	let	pull	this
am	fast	like	push	thought
an	father	little	put	through
and	feel	long	ran	time
any	find	look	read	to
are	first	lot	ride	together
around	floor	love	right	tomorrow
as	for	made	room	too
ask	found	make	run	took
at	friend	mama	said	try
baby	from	man	sat	turn
back	fun	may	saw	until
ball	gave	me	say	up
bath	get	mean	says	us
be	give	Miss	school	use
because	go	mom	see	very
bed	good	more	self	wait
began	got	morning	she	walk
best	grand	mother	shop	want
better	great	Mr.	should	was
big	had	Mrs.	shout	watch
blue	hand	my	side	way
body	hard	never	sister	we
boy	has	new	sit	well
brother	have	next	sleep	went
but	he	nice	so	were
by	head	night	some	what
came	help	no	soon	when
can	her	not	stay	where
car	here	now	still	while
come	him	of	stop	who
could	his	off	sure	why
cry	home	oh	surprise	will
dad	house	old	take	with
day	how	on	teacher	would
dear	hurry	one	tell	yes
did	I	only	thank	you
do	if	or	that	your
does	in	other	the	
dog	is	our	their	
don't	it	out	them	

reproducible page

Teaching Skills Through Writing Aloud

When "writing aloud" the teacher talks and thinks aloud as he or she writes on the chalkboard. The class offers suggestions for revising, editing, and changing whatever the teacher is writing on the chalkboard. Writing-aloud activities provide opportunities to teach a variety of writing conventions including punctuation, capitalization, grammar, sentence fragments, and inventive spellings. One way to do writing aloud is to start each day with a morning message on the chalkboard. Write a message on the board about something that is going to happen that day. Think aloud as you write. Look for opportunities to model writing throughout the learning day. The following activities provide opportunities for writing aloud.

Show students how you write. Demonstrate how you solve problems as you write.

School Family Picnic
May 15th is our school picnic. It

How should I write this?

Let's Edit

Write a sentence on the chalkboard that includes errors in punctuation, spelling, capitalization, and/or grammar. Then ask the class to help you find and correct the errors in the writing sample. After all corrections have been made, have students copy the sentence correctly in their writing notebooks.

Use Students' Writing Skills

Ask a student for permission to use some sentences from his/her writing to use for a class lesson. Write the sentences on the chalkboard and revise and edit them with the class.

Use samples of students' actual writing to teach editing.

My Writing Checklist

My name _____

My writing project _____

- [ ] My name is on my work.
- [ ] My work has a title.
- [ ] My handwriting is neat.
- [ ] Each sentence begins with a capital letter.
- [ ] Each sentence ends with correct punctuation.
- [ ] Each sentence is a complete thought.
- [ ] Each word is spelled correctly.
- [ ] _____
- [ ] _____
- [ ] _____

I feel _____ about the work I did on this project

because _____

_____

Teacher: On the blank lines, list other items you want students to check for. Have your students fill in this proofreading evaluation form after they complete a writing project.

Use Published Material to Teach Skills

Copy a well-written passage from literature on the chalkboard to show action, suspense, character descriptions, flashbacks, dialog, and beginnings and endings of stories. Your classroom library is a gold mine of well-written examples.

My Writing Checklist

Reproduce the checklist on **page 86** for students to use with writing projects.

Children learn by example. Expose them to well-written passages.

Using Journals in Your Writing Program

Journals can be notebooks, diaries, and/or learning logs.

Journal Formats

Add interest to journals by having a variety of journal formats for students. Some ideas are shown here.

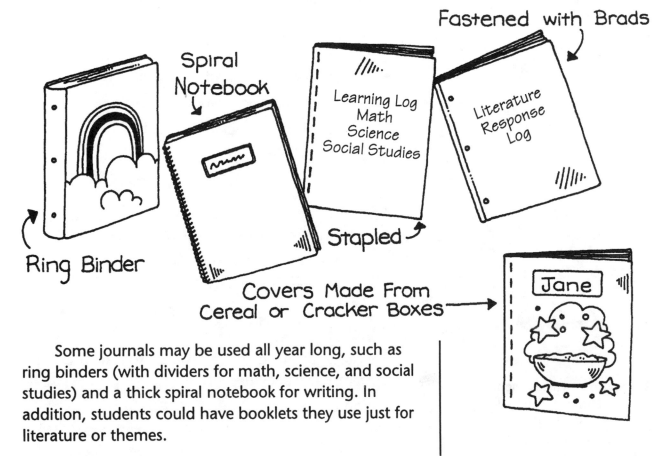

Fastened with Brads

Spiral Notebook

Learning Log Math Science Social Studies

Literature Response Log

Ring Binder

Stapled

Covers Made From Cereal or Cracker Boxes

Jane

Some journals may be used all year long, such as ring binders (with dividers for math, science, and social studies) and a thick spiral notebook for writing. In addition, students could have booklets they use just for literature or themes.

> Journals help students analyze, integrate, and synthesize information.

The Purpose of Journals

Recording in journals can help students analyze, integrate, and synthesize information.

When students analyze, they

- take information apart
- look at the bits and pieces

When students integrate and synthesize, they

- draw conclusions
- form inferences
- see relationships
- connect new and prior knowledge

How Journals Are Used by Students

Students can use journals to

- record information and observations
- organize ideas
- reach conclusions
- write about something they learned
- write and define a vocabulary word
- make a list of vocabulary words
- ask and answer an important question
- draw an illustration/chart/graph/diagram
- make predictions
- write what they already know about topic
- describe what they want to find out
- evaluate what they have learned
- list sources where they found or can find information
- write about field trips, resource speakers, experiments, and activities
- plan projects

> *Journals provide a rich medium for varied writing activities.*

Students can write on right pages and use pages on left for illustrations, charts, and diagrams.

Helping Students With Journal Writing

Take time to hold discussions with your class before asking students to write in their journals. Writing is much easier for students when they have an opportunity to think, talk, and listen to others first.

1. Group Discussion Before Journal Writing

Help your students learn to use journals effectively by holding group discussions prior to having them write individually. For example, if you want students to write a question they have about a topic, hold a class discussion first. Elicit questions from the class, list questions on the chalkboard, then ask students to write one of their own questions in their individual journals.

2. Partner Sharing

Hold a group discussion, then have students tell a partner what they are going to write in their individual journals. Then have students write. Talking first about what you plan to write makes writing easier for virtually all students.

3. Planning Projects on Paper

Planning projects and activities in journals helps students use writing as an organizational tool. For example, have students list the steps they will take and sketch how finished project will look.

Take time to prepare students for writing.

Journals are a great tool for planning projects.

Using Journals in Grades K–1

Work together using a group journal in grades K–1. Group journals provide opportunities to link listening, talking, reading, and writing. You are also modeling journal writing for your students. Simply staple together a big blank book to use as a journal. Elicit sentences from your class to write in your class/group journal. You can have group journals for science, math, themes, and literature.

> Expose beginning writers to group journals.

Feb. 24
We learned about mammals today. They
- have hair
- nurse their babies
-

are warm-blooded

Using Journals With Read-Aloud Books

See **Chapter 2, pages 24–25**, for ideas on connecting journals with books teachers read aloud to their students.

Letter Writing— A Practical Writing Activity

Writing group or individual letters for a purpose demonstrates to students that writing is practical and is used throughout our lives.

Dictated group letters provide opportunities to teach mini-lessons on writing skills.

> Letter writing provides a practical application of skills.

1. Dictated Group Letters

Have the class dictate sentences for a group letter in grades K–6. Record students' sentences on chart paper and have all students sign the letter. Here are a few appropriate opportunities to write group letters:

- Welcome parents to open house.
- Thank people who help in your classroom.
- Express thanks to resource speakers.
- Communicate information to other classes.
- Express get-well wishes to someone.
- Congratulate someone.
- Request information.
- Ask for assistance.
- Write to pen-pal classes.

Group letters are appropriate for any grade level.

2. Individual Letters

Students can write individual letters for the same purposes listed for dictated group letters.

A letter-writing form is provided on page 92.

Dear Dr. Gomez,   Nov. 6

Thanks for visiting our class. We learned a lot about being a veterinarian. We will take care of the cat skeleton you let us borrow.

We all learned how to take care of our pets.

Sincerely,

Sarah   Patti
                    Ms. Green
Paul   Jason

Stephan   Julie

A Note of Thanks

Date _____

Dear _____ ,

_____

_____

_____

_____

_____

Sincerely,

_____

Notes and Messages in Your Classroom

Note writing is another real writing activity that students seem to enjoy.

1. Message Board

Start a message board in your classroom. Simply provide paper for messages, an area on a bulletin board, and pushpins for posting messages. Students can jot a message and post it on the board for others to read. You will find that students enjoy reading messages and posting responses to other students' messages.

Children enjoy reading and writing notes and messages.

2. Share Your Thoughts

Place a large piece of paper on a table or counter-top in your classroom. Write a question across the paper and encourage your students to share their thoughts. Sample questions:

- What kinds of books do you like best? Why?
- What do you like to do for fun on weekends?
- What do you usually do after school?
- What kinds of animals do you think make the best pets? Why?
- What do you like best about school? Why?
- If you had $100 to spend, what would you do with the money?

Sharing ideas can be a springboard for writing.

On weekends, I like to . . .

work in my garden
Mrs. Beal

play soccer
Tyler

Connecting Writing and Literature

Connect writing and literature with the ideas in **Chapter 4.**

Helping Students Write Well

Writing is a risk-taking venture. In classrooms where there is a climate of trust and support, students can freely express ideas and feelings verbally and in writing.

Teachers need to take time to develop concepts with students before asking them to write. Prepare for writing through the five-step process described below. In it, students are given time to explore and develop ideas instead of rushing into writing unprepared. This strategy can be applied to all your favorite writing topics. It will help your students write with greater depth and richer in detail.

Step 1: Topic Presentation—Teacher announces the topic. For example, writing about our opinions.

Step 2: Teacher Disclosure—The teacher shares some of her/his opinions by making a few "I think" statements.

Let's talk about some of our opinions. I think it's a good idea to have a vegetable garden.

Step 3: Class Discussion—Have students who wish to share tell the class some of their opinions through "I think" statements.

I think camping is the best kind of vacation.

I think cats are the best pets.

I think soccer is the best sport.

Writing is easier when there are opportunities to develop concepts before beginning to write.

Discussing and sharing opinions helps a concept take shape.

Step 4: Partner Sharing—Have each student tell a partner an "I think" statement and explain why he holds that opinion.

They don't make loud sounds like dogs. And, cats keep themselves very clean.

Step 5: Individual Writing—Students proceed on their own to develop their ideas by writing "I think" statements and opinions.

"I think" statements help students focus their thoughts.

Helping Students Write Descriptively

Begin by asking students to find a rock that is not larger than their fists. Have students place their rocks on their desks. Conduct a class discussion about the rocks, asking students to describe them. Focus on colors, shapes, and textures. List adjectives about the rocks on the chalkboard. Have students draw detailed, colored illustrations of their individual rocks. Ask students to list adjectives under their illustrations that can be used to describe their rocks. Then have students tell a partner where they found their rocks and why they chose them. Now that you have held class and partner discussions, have students write paragraphs about their rocks telling where their specimens were found, why they were chosen, and what the rocks look like.

Encourage descriptive writing by letting students observe color, shape, size, texture, and other properties.

Have books available about geology and rocks. Students can try to identify their rocks. Have students set up a geology display.

Another way of helping students write more descriptively is to divide the class into groups and give each group a flower. Flowers should all be the same type. Have a class discussion about the flowers, describing shape, color, fragrance, petals, stems, and leaves. Have students draw a detailed illustration of the flower and write descriptive sentences. Students enjoy drawing labeled illustrations. (Fruit can be used instead of flowers for this activity. Give each group an apple, or use one pineapple for the whole class.) In K–1 classrooms, adjectives and sentences can be dictated by students for teachers to write on the chalkboard.

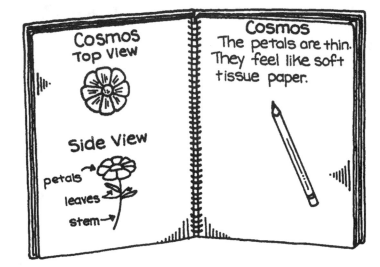

Holding Conferences About Writing

Conferences give students valuable feedback about their writing. The process of getting and giving feedback helps students become skillful writers.

Kinds of Conferences

Through conferences students can receive feedback on their writing and discuss ways to improve their writing. Conferences about writing can be held between:

- teacher and student
- pairs of students
- small groups of students
- whole class and a writer

Give students opportunities to observe both living and nonliving things.

Conferences provide opportunities to give and receive feedback on writing.

Tips to Enhance Writing Conferences

These tips will help you and your students make the most of writing conferences.

1. Prior to the writing conference, tell students to read their writing aloud to themselves. When students hear their words, they often catch errors they would have missed visually. This is the way professional proofreaders read manuscripts.

2. After a student reads his writing aloud, have someone read it aloud to the author. This gives writers an opportunity to hear their work.

3. Remind students to give feedback in a positive way. Tell students to offer feedback that includes:

- a positive comment
- a suggestion for improvement
- another positive comment

(Criticism is sandwiched between positive comments.)

4. Post a list of writing partners and/or writing groups on the chalkboard. Every three or four weeks reassign partners and groups. Assigning students ahead of time helps you get students into groups quickly and easily.

Feedback is an important tool for improving writing skills.

The boy was all along…whoops…it should be alone.

Teacher and Student Conferences

Keep records of writing conferences with students in a spiral notebook. Clip a class list on the cover of the book. A reproducible class-record form is on the following page. Place masking-tape tabs with students' names throughout the book, allowing four or five pages per student.

When you have a writing conference with a student, write the date and jot comments in that student's section of the book. If you do so once a week, by the end of the year you will have recorded approximately three dozen dated comments. Share your writing records with parents at conferences. You can remove each student's section of the notebook and add them to students' portfolios.

Teacher-Student Conferences

Hold short two- to three-minute conferences with students. Ask questions that focus on the actual writing and ask students to evaluate their own writing. Suggested questions/topics include these:

Tell me about your writing.

What will you write next?

What do you do best as a writer?

What would improve your writing?

What is the best part of this piece?

How does this compare with your . . . other story? . . . writing from yesterday? . . . writing from last week?

Written Feedback From Teachers to Students

In addition to discussing the student's writing directly with the student, you can provide written feedback. Affix a stick-on note to the student's paper or use one of the reproducible forms on **pages 100–101.**

Stay in touch with students' writing through conferences.

Encourage students to evaluate their own writing as well as having others evaluate it.

Record Sheet for

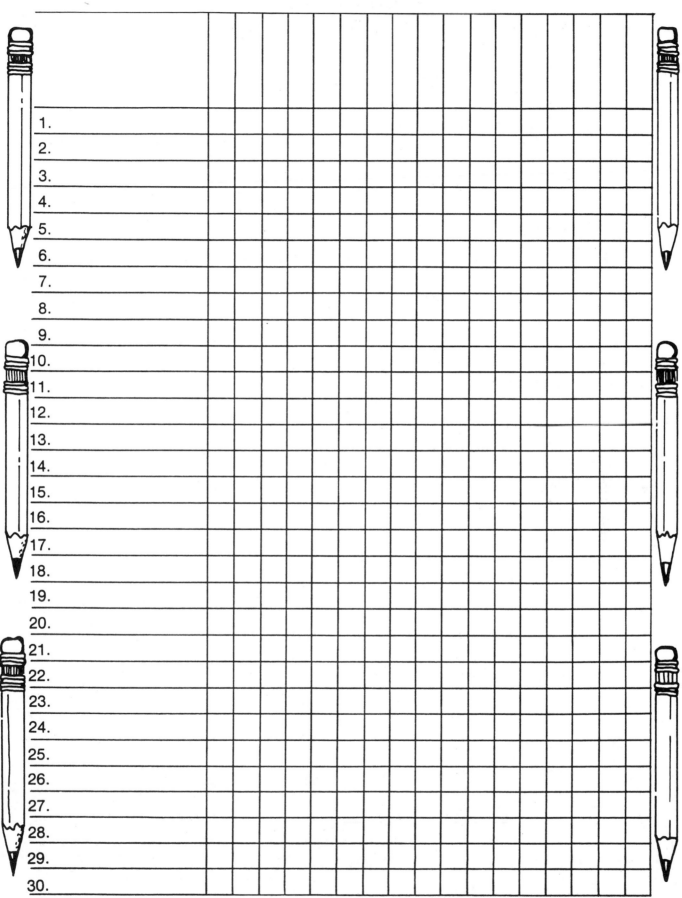

1.
2.
3.
4.
5.
6.
7.
8.
9.
10.
11.
12.
13.
14.
15.
16.
17.
18.
19.
20.
21.
22.
23.
24.
25.
26.
27.
28.
29.
30.

reproducible page

Writer's Name _____

The strong points of your paper are _____

_____

_____

Your paper can be improved by _____

_____

_____

From _____ Date _____

Writing Conference Report

Date _____ Writer_____

Name of reader _____

As a reader, I liked _____

_____

_____

I suggest _____

_____

_____

FS-8128 *100% Practical*

Reader Response Form

Reader's name _____

Writer's name _____

Date _____

I like this paper because

_____

_____

_____

_____

My ideas for improving this paper are

_____

_____

_____

_____

These changes should be made because

_____

_____

_____

_____

FS-8128 *100% Practical*

Partner and small-group conferences are a non-threatening way to provide feedback on writing.

Reader
Read your writing aloud.

Summarizer
I heard you say . . .
Your writing is about . . .

Questioner
Tell me more about . . .
Will you explain . . .

Suggester
Think about what people in your group said. Make a suggestion to the writer.

Praiser
I liked . . .
My favorite part . . .

Observer
Make sure everyone gets a turn.

Partner Conferences

Pairs of students can share their writing and offer verbal feedback. Students can also provide written feedback using the forms on **pages 100–101**.

Small-Group Conferences

Small groups are ideal for conferences. They furnish opportunities for feedback from more than one source while allowing the writer freedom from feeling overwhelmed. Here are some ideas for holding conferences in small groups.

1. One student in the group reads his writing aloud while others listen and provide feedback on one of the forms on page 100. Then the reader collects written feedback from members of the group. Students continue taking turns reading their writing aloud.

2. Divide students into groups of three for this conferencing activity. One student reads his writing aloud to the other two group members, who are listeners. Listeners read the paper silently and comment on the writing. Then a different student takes a turn as the reader. Continue until all three students have had an opportunity to read their writing aloud and receive verbal feedback.

3. Make up sets of cards for this conference activity. Group students into sections of five or six. Give each group a set of cards. Students pass out the cards so each student knows his role. After one student has taken his turn as "Reader" and other students have responded as shown on their cards, students pass the cards. Now a different student takes a turn as "Reader." If you have groups of only five students, eliminate the role of "Observer."

Whole-Class Conferencing With Writers

Many students enjoy being "in the spotlight." One positive way to achieve this is to set aside a special chair as the "Reader's Chair" or "Author's Chair."

You can have one student read his writing aloud to the class from this special chair. (It takes a lot of time to let every student read aloud to the whole class. Don't try to have too many students do this at one sitting or the audience can get restless.) Invite one or two students at a time to take the Author's Chair. Keep track of students who have had a turn. Over time make sure all students who want to share their work with the whole class have a chance to do so.

You can increase interest and improve pacing by asking the class questions after a writer reads his work aloud from the Author's Chair. Ask the class, "What was the writing about?" Elicit a response and then quickly ask another question like, "What did you enjoy about it?" or "Does anyone have a suggestion to make this writing even better?"

Another idea that works especially well with older students is to ask them to prepare a question for the writer, or have the writer prepare questions he or she would like the audience to respond to about the writing. (Example: "Did I use enough descriptive words for you to clearly picture the character of Spike?")

An "Author's Chair" can spotlight a student's efforts.

Keep Writing!

You'll find more writing activities in the chapters listed below and throughout this book.

Chapter 4 Reading and Using Literature

Chapter 6 Classroom Publishing

Chapter 8 Using Themes

Make writing a part of every day.

Students need time to think about and talk about topics before they write. Also, writers need an environment where they will find support and encouragement. Look for ways to weave writing into classroom activities throughout the learning day.

NOTES

Publish It

Publishing is an exciting activity for all grade levels. Your students will enjoy writing and publishing three kinds of books in your classroom:

- Class Books (each student creates one page)
- Group Books
- Individual Books

Directions for making interesting books in varied formats appear on **pages 216–221** in **Chapter 11**. Copy and laminate the directions and have them available at your publishing center for student reference.

Classroom Publishing Center

Take a look at the Classroom Publishing Center in **Chapter 9** on **page 188**. Your publishing center can be a place where students obtain materials for publishing. Then they work on their publishing activities away from the center. Or, if you have adequate space, you can set up a center where students do the work.

Writing Class Books

The whole class works together to make one book in this publishing endeavor. Class books are an excellent way to teach students about publishing. Later, when students work in publishing groups or work individually, they will use their experience to succeed. Class books can be placed in the classroom library. At the end of the year they can be given away as prizes or un-stapled and individual pages returned to students.

Class books can be fastened with staples, binder rings, or brads. To make a class book extra-special, insert students' pages into a magnetic photo album.

The classroom is the perfect setting for publishing.

Create a publishing center in your classroom.

Everyone can participate in making a class book for all to enjoy.

Class books can be made on just about any subject.

Class Books About Literature

After reading a story aloud to your class, have your students make a book about the story.

Ask every student to draw a picture about the story on 12" x 18" paper. Students can add a caption to their pictures, or dictate sentences for you to write. Compile pages into a class book.

Publishing a Commemorative Book About Literature

This marvelous class-publishing activity is described in **Chapter 2,** "Reading Aloud," on **page 21.**

Books About Class Activities

Have your class make a book about a special event such as a book fair, resource speaker, or field trip. Discuss the event or activity, then have every student create one page for the class book. Students draw a picture and write or dictate sentences. Compile pages into a book.

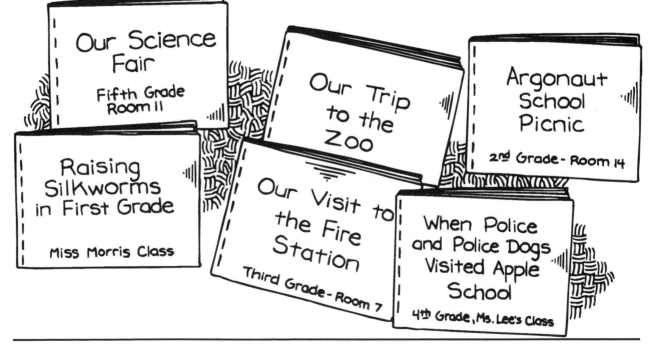

Books About Out-of-School Activities

Have each student make a picture and write sentences about favorite weekend activities, pets, or something they did over vacation. Compile pages into class books.

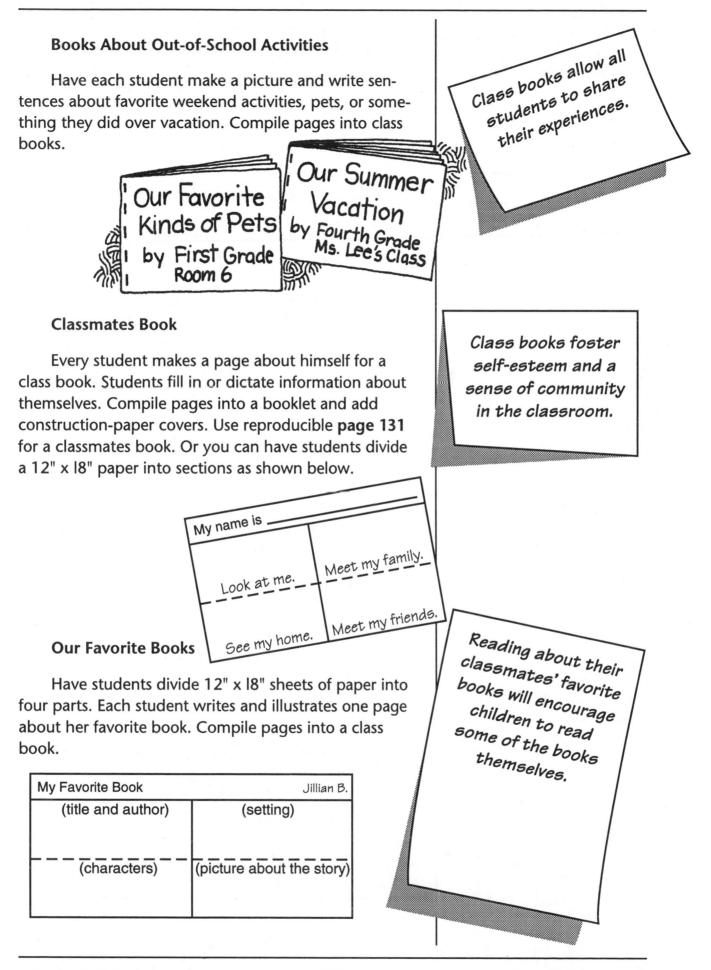

Class books allow all students to share their experiences.

Classmates Book

Every student makes a page about himself for a class book. Students fill in or dictate information about themselves. Compile pages into a booklet and add construction-paper covers. Use reproducible **page 131** for a classmates book. Or you can have students divide a 12" x 18" paper into sections as shown below.

Class books foster self-esteem and a sense of community in the classroom.

My name is _____

Look at me.

See my home.

Meet my family.

Meet my friends.

Our Favorite Books

Have students divide 12" x 18" sheets of paper into four parts. Each student writes and illustrates one page about her favorite book. Compile pages into a class book.

Reading about their classmates' favorite books will encourage children to read some of the books themselves.

My Favorite Book	Jillian B.
(title and author)	(setting)
(characters)	(picture about the story)

Class Poetry Books

Compile students' poems into a book. For example, if students are writing haiku poems, have each student choose his best piece for the class book.

One Day in Our Classroom

This book will become a favorite in your classroom library. Bring your camera to school. On a day when all students are present, snap a roll of film from the moment students enter the room in the morning until they leave at the end of the day. Make sure every student is in at least one picture. Take pictures of all the important aspects of the day, including some of your students eating lunches and on the playground.

When the photographs are developed, paste each one on a piece of 12" x 18" construction paper. Ask the class to suggest sentences or captions to write on each page about the photographs. Then spread the pages out along the chalk ledge. Have your students help you arrange the pages from left to right in chronological sequence. Add covers and make a book.

A variation on this activity is to make a book called "One Day at Our School," and include events that occur all around the campus instead of in the classroom.

Even everyday events are worth publishing.

Here's a snapshot of a day in your classroom—preserved in a class book.

Our class enjoys playing basketball.

9" x 12" or 12" x 18"

ABC Books

ABC books complement many topics and are perfect as culminating activities for themes. Write the topic on the chalkboard and list the alphabet vertically. Then elicit from students a word or words that relates to the topic for the letters of the alphabet. Assign each student to a different letter to make a page for the ABC Book. Assemble the pages in alphabetical order, add covers, and fasten into a book.

Class books are as easy as ABC!

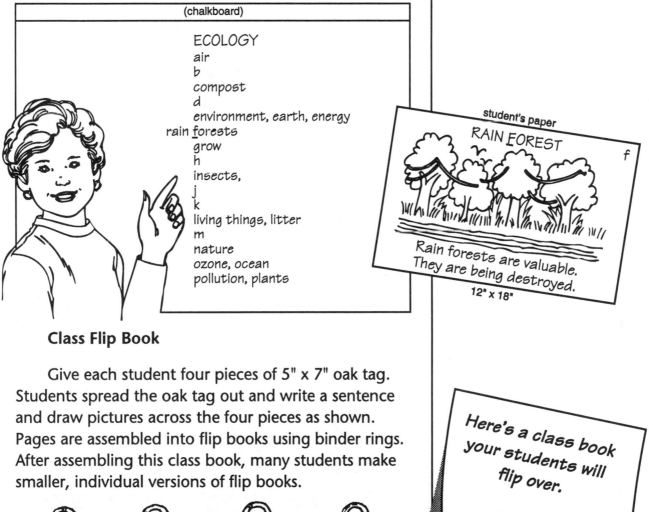

(chalkboard)

ECOLOGY
air
b
compost
d
environment, earth, energy
rain forests
grow
h
insects,
j
k
living things, litter
m
nature
ozone, ocean
pollution, plants

student's paper
RAIN FOREST   f

Rain forests are valuable.
They are being destroyed.
12" x 18"

Class Flip Book

Give each student four pieces of 5" x 7" oak tag. Students spread the oak tag out and write a sentence and draw pictures across the four pieces as shown. Pages are assembled into flip books using binder rings. After assembling this class book, many students make smaller, individual versions of flip books.

Here's a class book your students will flip over.

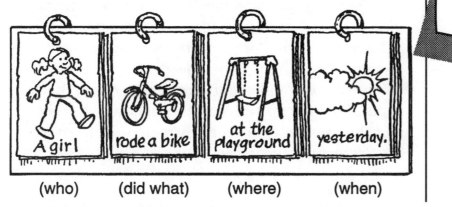

A girl	rode a bike	at the playground	yesterday.
(who)	(did what)	(where)	(when)

Writing Group Books

Groups work cooperatively to make one book.

Reader's Scrapbook

After your class reads a work of literature, divide the class into groups. Have each group create a book about the work. Books should include writing and illustrations as shown below.

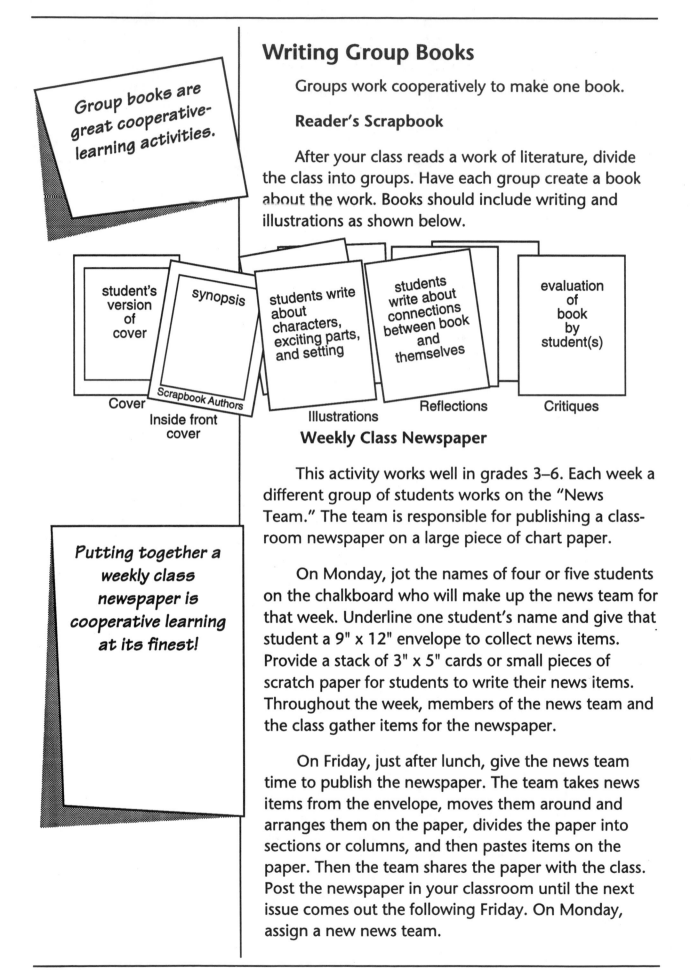

Group books are great cooperative-learning activities.

| student's version of cover | synopsis | students write about characters, exciting parts, and setting | students write about connections between book and themselves | evaluation of book by student(s) |

Scrapbook Authors

Cover

Inside front cover

Illustrations

Reflections

Critiques

Weekly Class Newspaper

This activity works well in grades 3–6. Each week a different group of students works on the "News Team." The team is responsible for publishing a classroom newspaper on a large piece of chart paper.

On Monday, jot the names of four or five students on the chalkboard who will make up the news team for that week. Underline one student's name and give that student a 9" x 12" envelope to collect news items. Provide a stack of 3" x 5" cards or small pieces of scratch paper for students to write their news items. Throughout the week, members of the news team and the class gather items for the newspaper.

On Friday, just after lunch, give the news team time to publish the newspaper. The team takes news items from the envelope, moves them around and arranges them on the paper, divides the paper into sections or columns, and then pastes items on the paper. Then the team shares the paper with the class. Post the newspaper in your classroom until the next issue comes out the following Friday. On Monday, assign a new news team.

Putting together a weekly class newspaper is cooperative learning at its finest!

The first time you do a weekly class newspaper, collect the news items yourself. On Friday let the whole class discuss how the paper should be organized. Publishing one issue of the newspaper as a whole-class activity teaches students what to do when they work independently in groups.

After you get them started, the students take over all the work.

36" x 36"

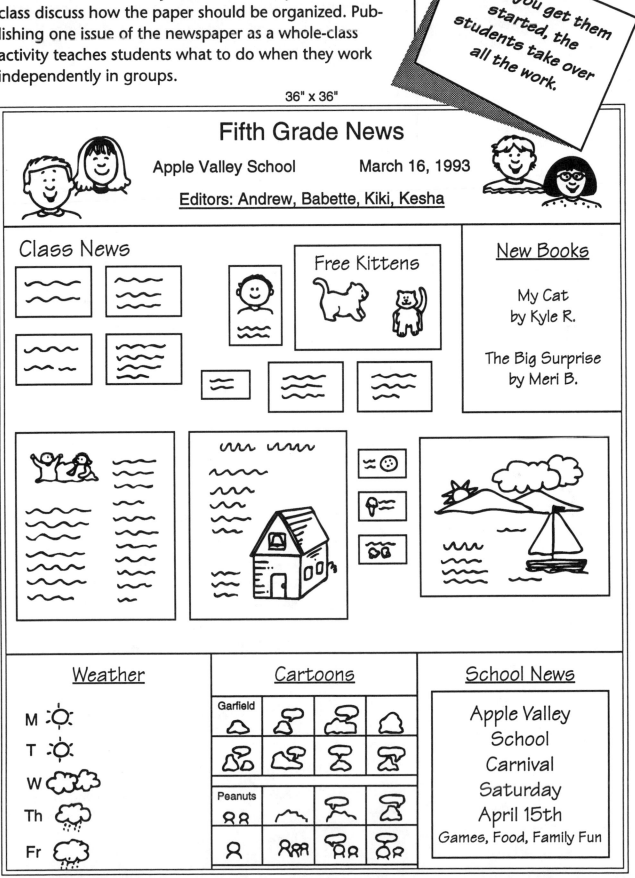

Fifth Grade News

Apple Valley School   March 16, 1993

Editors: Andrew, Babette, Kiki, Kesha

Class News

Free Kittens

New Books

My Cat
by Kyle R.

The Big Surprise
by Meri B.

Weather

M ☼
T ☼
W ☁
Th ☁
Fr ☁

Cartoons

Garfield

Peanuts

School News

Apple Valley
School
Carnival
Saturday
April 15th
Games, Food, Family Fun

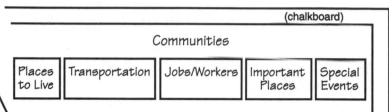

Make class books with social studies and science themes.

Cooperative Book Project About Themes

This activity is perfect as a culminating whole-class activity for science or social-studies themes. Write the name of the theme on the chalkboard. Elicit from students important subtopics the class learned about during the theme study.

		(chalkboard)

Communities

Places to Live	Transportation	Jobs/Workers	Important Places	Special Events

Divide the class into groups and assign each group a subtopic. Each group creates a section or chapter for the class book. When sections are completed, have groups share the pages they have created. Then hold a class discussion about compiling the book. The class will need to decide the sequence of the chapters. Other items to be added include covers, a title page, table of contents, and page numbers.

Student's-Choice Books

Elicit from your class five or six high-interest topics for books. Draw five or six lines for students' names under each topic, making sure you have enough lines for all the students in your class. Let students take turns signing up to work on a book. When everyone has joined a "book group," have the sections meet to discuss what kinds of information they might want to include in their books. Take the class to the school library to gather books and information about the topics. Each group creates a book with writing and illustrations. Then the groups share completed books with the class before placing them in the classroom library.

			(chalkboard)

Topics for Nonfiction Books

Sharks	Prehistoric Animals	Earthquakes	49er's Team	Whales
1. ___	1. _____	1. _____	1. _____	1. ___
2. ___	2. _____	2. _____	2. _____	2. ___
3. ___	3. _____	3. _____	3. _____	3. ___
4. ___	4. _____	4. _____	4. _____	4. ___
5. ___	5. _____	5. _____	5. _____	5. ___

Writing Individual Books

Over a period of time, hold class discussions to give students an opportunity to analyze and discuss different aspects of book production.

Collect a group of books and focus attention on their covers. Compare and contrast the covers, asking students what attracts to them to certain ones. Display the books for students to look at after your class discussion. On another occasion, hold a discussion about different media that are used to illustrate books. These discussions about books will help students carefully consider the many aspects of designing and writing original books. You can focus on these aspects at different times.

- covers
- art media
- dedication
- "about the author"
- sizes and shapes
- page design (how text and illustrations are arranged on the page)

Explore all parts of a book with your students.

Helping Students Sequence Pages

Students can use the chalk ledge to arrange their pages into the correct sequence before fastening books together. Chalk-ledge sequencing is explained on **page 22** in **Chapter 2**.

Patterned-language books make good models for beginning writers.

Ideas for Individual Books

Repeating-Pattern Book—Teach a class lesson on how to make a book. Read aloud a book that has a repetitive pattern. Change the book's pattern slightly and make a reproducible form. You can print the pattern on an 8½" x 11" paper. Students can fill in the missing word and make an illustration on the top half of each page.

You can also print the pattern two times on a reproducible form, reproduce, and cut into strips. Students paste the pattern on a piece of art paper, fill in the missing word, and illustrate the page.

Students can have any number of pages in their books. This easy publishing project gives students an opportunity to have fun making a book they will enjoy reading again and again.

> *Younger students especially enjoy making cut-and-paste books. They get practice with scissors skills, too!*

Funny bunny, funny bunny
What do you see?
I see a _____
looking at me.

8¹/₂" x 11" reproducible

8¹/₂" x 11" reproducible — student writes a word

Funny bunny, funny bunny
What do you see?
I see a _____
looking at me.

student pastes strip on art paper, writes missing word and makes an illustration.

Books About Books—Have your students create books about books. See the ideas for making books about works of literature in **Chapter 2, page 25-26.**

"All Through the Year" Book—Start this project at the beginning of the year. Students will complete two pages of the book each month of the school year. At some time during the first month of school, have students make an 11-page booklet. You can use the reproducibles on **pages 115–117** for this book or simply have students write the names of the months on the pages. Students perform a writing activity about the month on the right-hand page and make a picture on the left-hand page. Collect the books and return them to students the next month to add an activity for that month. At the end of the year, students can take completed books home.

> *Students will enjoy adding a decorative art theme to each month's activity.*

All Through the Year

by

_____

September

October

reproducible page

FS-8128 *100% Practical*

reproducible page

reproducible page

FS-8128 *100% Practical*

Origami Books—This paper-folding activity results in an eight-page origami book. The books can be made in many sizes and shapes. Directions for folding origami books appear below. Make books as a class activity a few times first, then post the directions for students to follow later on their own.

Students can learn to make these cleverly folded books on their own.

Ideas for contents of origami books:

- riddles
- all about me
- my friends
- my family
- picture dictionary
- poetry
- seasons
- all about my pet
- phonics
- colors

Sizes of origami books

Size of paper	Size of finished book
8½" x 11"	2¾" x 4¼"
12" x 18"	4½" x 6"
18" x 24"	6" x 9"

Origami Book Directions:

1. Fold a sheet of paper (any size) into eighths (Fig. 1). Unfold.

   Fig.1

2. Refold halfway. (Fig. 2)

   Fig.2

3. Cut on middle fold halfway in. (Fig. 3)

   Fig.3

4. When open, it should have a slit through the middle. (Fig. 4)

   1st   4th
   slit would be here
   Fig.4

5. Fold in half lengthwise and push ends in toward middle. (Fig. 5)

   Fig.5

6. Push until first and fourth fold meet and flop over. (Fig. 6)

   Fig.6

7. Will end up as a book with eight pages to write on.

   Fig.7

Monday-to-Friday Books—Students can create five-page books during a week at school by creating one page each day, then compiling the pages into a book. To make a book about pets, jot a different sentence starter on the chalkboard each day of the week. Students copy and complete the sentence and make a colorful illustration about the sentence. At the end of the week students have five illustrated pages. They can add covers, a title page, and decorations to make their books special.

Children will look forward to doing a page each day for Monday-to-Friday books.

All About My Pet

Monday: I have (or wish I had) a _____
        as a pet because . . .

Tuesday: My pet's name is . . .

Wednesday: I got my pet . . .

Thursday: My pet likes to . . .

Friday: My pet is funny when . . .

Other Ideas for Monday-to-Friday Books

School Days

I'm in . . . grade in room . . .

My teacher is . . .

My favorite subject is . . .

At school I look forward to . . .

My classroom is . . .

I have a dog as a pet because I love animals.

My pet's name is Muffy.

I got my pet at the animal shelter.

My pet likes to chase squirrels.

My pet is funny when she sleeps on her back.

Here are some other ideas for Monday-to-Friday Books:

School Days

The best thing about my grade is . . .

My teacher is . . .

My favorite subject is . . .

At school I look forward to . . .

My classroom is . . .

Away From Home

I stayed overnight at . . .

The fun part was . . .

I slept in . . .

I missed my . . .

Next time, I . . .

Weekend Fun

The best thing about weekends is . . .

The worst thing about weekends is . . .

On Saturdays I like to . . .

On Sundays I like to . . .

On weekends I go to bed at . . .

Growing Up

When I'm grown I want to work . . .

When I'm an adult I'd like to live . . .

The best thing about being an adult is . . .

The worst thing about being an adult is . . .

I'll be the kind of adult who . . .

Stormy Weather

My favorite kind of weather is . . .

The weather I like least is . . .

Storms sometimes . . .

During stormy weather I like to . . .

I remember a storm when . . .

My Friend

My best friend is . . .

We like to . . .

My friend lives . . .

My friend and I are alike because . . .

We are different because . . .

Little Books

Have your whole class make a little book together to teach students how to use this format for publishing. Then provide a variety of book formats at your publishing center. Students can choose a format for creating a book. Reproducible "little book" formats follow on **pages 121–125**. The format on **page 125** does not have a title so students can create books about topics of their own choosing.

The whole class can make little books together.

1 That's What Friends Are For by _____	**2** Friends_____ _____
3 Friends_____ _____	**4** Friends_____ _____
5 Friends_____ _____	**6** My friend is _____ We like to _____ _____ That's what friends are for.

FS-8128 *100% Practical*

1

All About My School

by _____

2

My school _____

_____

3

I like to _____

_____

4

At School _____

_____

5

At recess I _____

_____

6

My teacher _____

_____

1

My Family

by _____

2

Meet my family.

3

We live _____

_____

4

We like to _____

_____

5

We _____

_____

6

My family is _____

_____

FS-8128 *100% Practical*

1

Pets Are Special

by ____________________

2

Meet my pets.

3

My pet likes to ____________

____

4

My pet makes me laugh.

5

Pets are ________________

____

6

Pets are special because ______

____

reproducible page

by

_____

 FS-8128 *100% Practical*

> Student editors and art directors make publishing more interesting and successful.

Writing and Publishing Original Storybooks

Involve your whole class in this publishing activity. Your students will be proud of the books they create.

Step 1. Tell students they get to write and illustrate a book. Give students a few days to think about the books they will write.

Step 2. Have students write a summary of the book they plan to write. Ask them to write sentences telling about the beginning, middle, and end. Next, have students give their books a title. Writing a summary and title before writing the book helps students organize their thoughts and write cohesive stories.

Step 3. Assign all students to an editor and an art director. Every student writes his own book, edits a classmate's book, and is art director for another classmate's book. Post a class list at the publishing center listing editors and art directors.

Step 4. Students write their first drafts.

Step 5. Writers read their stories to their editors. Then editors read the stories back so writers can hear their stories read aloud. Then writers and editors confer on ways to improve the writing.

Step 6. Writers make revisions.

Step 7. Writers confer with the teacher.

Step 8. Writers complete their final copies.

Step 9. Writers cut apart their stories and paste sentences across pages of the book. Students number the pages of their manuscripts.

Step 10. Writers meet with their art directors to discuss the illustrations they plan to draw.

Step 11. Writers illustrate their stories.

Step 12. Writers add finishing touches to their books such as title page covers and an About the Author section. (About the Author/Dedication reproducibles are provided on **page 127**.)

About the Author

_____

_____

_____

_____

_____

_____

_____

_____

About the Author

_____

_____

_____

_____

This book is dedicated to

_____

I wish to thank these people for their help:

_____

_____

_____

_____

This book is dedicated to

_____

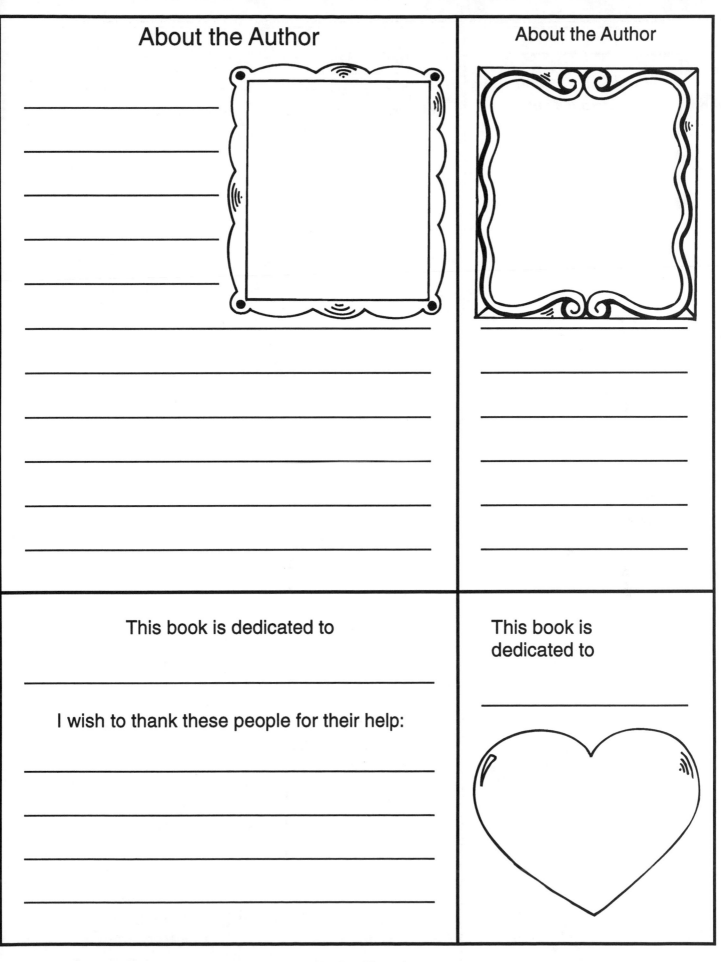

FS-8128 *100% Practical*

Book Jackets

Students can create book jackets for their books. They can have a few classmates read their stories and provide written comments about the stories. Testimonials about students' books can be copied or pasted on the book jackets.

Book jackets can entice children to read.

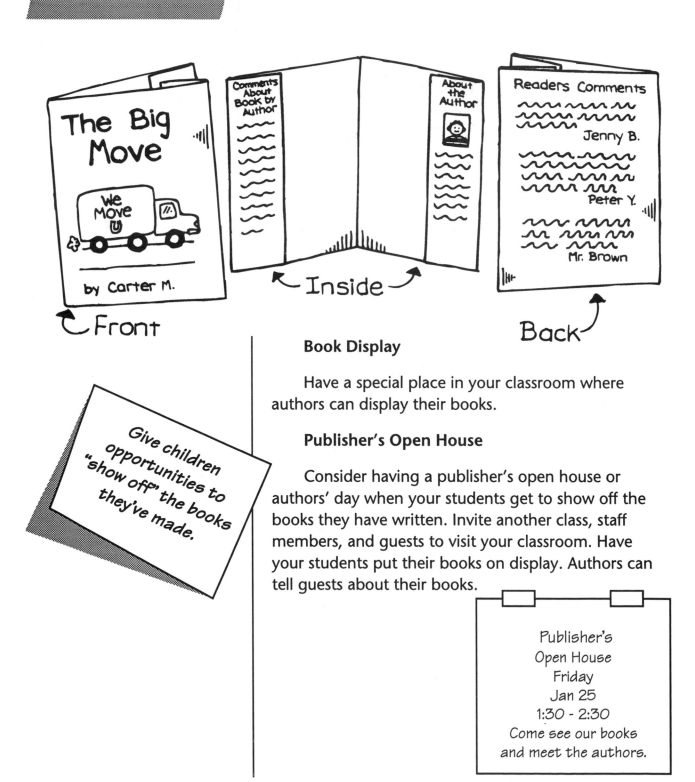

Book Display

Have a special place in your classroom where authors can display their books.

Publisher's Open House

Consider having a publisher's open house or authors' day when your students get to show off the books they have written. Invite another class, staff members, and guests to visit your classroom. Have your students put their books on display. Authors can tell guests about their books.

Give children opportunities to "show off" the books they've made.

Publisher's
Open House
Friday
Jan 25
1:30 - 2:30
Come see our books
and meet the authors.

Monitoring Students' Progress in Publishing

You can know at a glance exactly which step of the publishing process students are on by using the magnet chart described in **Chapter 9** on **page 165**.

Publishing
Write First Copy
Meet with Editor
Revise your story ⊖⊖⊖⊖⊖⊖⊖
Meet with Teacher ⊖⊖⊖⊖
Write Final Copy ⊖⊖⊖⊖⊖⊖⊖
Meet with Art Director ⊖⊖⊖⊖⊖
Illustrate Your Book ⊖⊖⊖⊖

Charts help you and your students see progress at a glance.

Tracking Form for Publishing Progress

Instead of, or in addition to, using magnets as above, you can give each student a tracking form to record progress. Students can keep this form in their publishing folders. They would use a new form for each book they publish.

This form can be taken home when books are finished. It informs parents of the publishing process in your classroom. A reproducible tracking form appears on the following page.

Be sure to provide an organized place for "Work-in-Progress"

Storing Work in Progress

Furnish a box at your publishing center for student folders. Have each student keep a folder in which to store in-progress publishing projects. Hanging folders work especially well for this. Books-in-progress can also be stored in the "Box-it Storage System" shown on **page 188** in **Chapter 9**.

Classroom publishing is a valuable way to integrate reading, writing, and a host of other skills. Include it often in your program .

Publishing Checklist

1. I started my book on (date) _____ .

2. My book's title is:_____ .

3. My first copy was done on (date) _____ .

4. I met with my editor on (date) _____ .

   My editor is _____ .

5. If necessary, I revised my story.

6. I met with my teacher. (T) _____ (date) _____ .

7. My final copy was done on (date) _____ .

8. I met with my art director on (date) _____ .

   My art director is _____ .

9. I illustrated my story.

10. ☐ Title Page   ☐ Page Numbers

    ☐ Dedication   ☐ Book Jacket

    ☐ About the Author   ☐ _____

11. My book was done on (date) _____ .

My name is _____

All About Me

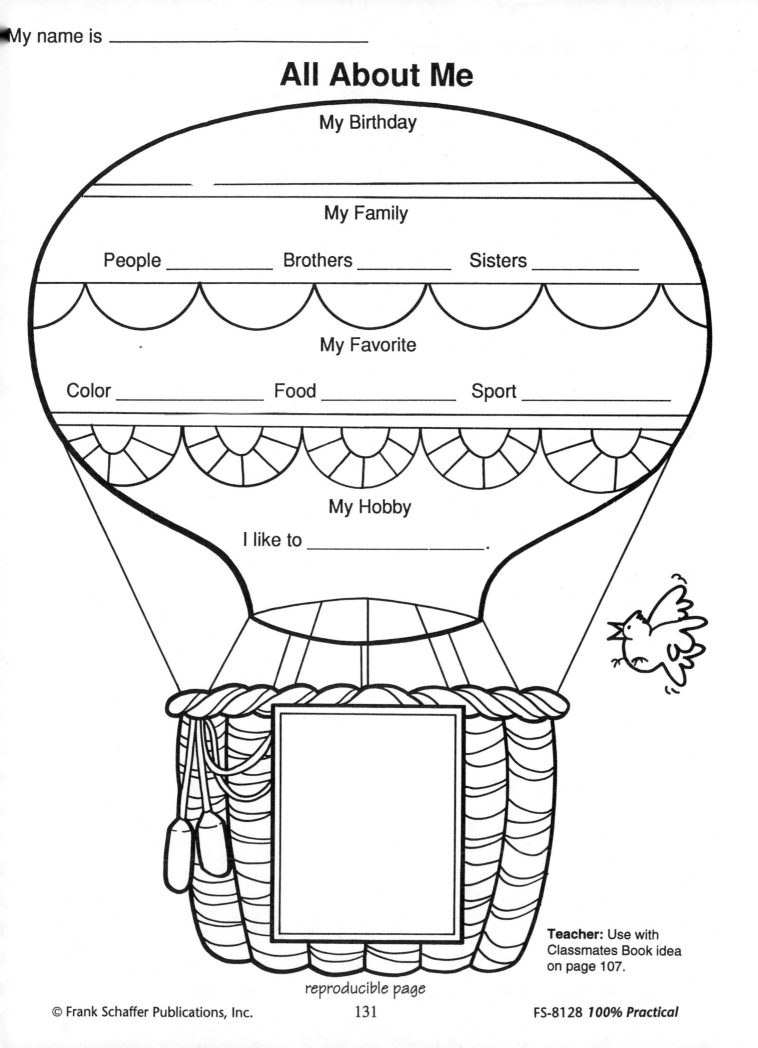

My Birthday

_____

My Family

People _____ Brothers _____ Sisters _____

My Favorite

Color _____ Food _____ Sport _____

My Hobby

I like to _____.

Teacher: Use with Classmates Book idea on page 107.

reproducible page

131   FS-8128 *100% Practical*

NOTES

Incorporating Oral Language

Weave oral-language experiences through writing and reading activities throughout the day. Offer activities that focus specifically on oral language as listed below.

My Own Tape

Use a blank audio-cassette tape for each student. Label tapes with students' names. Students can record a variety of oral-language activities on their tapes. Students should state the date each time they record. Try the idea for setting up a "Listen and Learn Center" on **page 176** in **Chapter 9.**

Post an activity for the week at the tape center. At the end of the year, let students take their audio tapes home. Activities suitable for audio taping include:

- Reading aloud from a reading book
- Reading an original poem aloud
- Reading an original story aloud
- Interviewing the teacher
- Interviewing a classmate
- Telling about your favorite leisure activity
- Telling about your pet
- Telling about your family
- Telling about your best friend
- Telling about a field trip
- Telling about a theme of study

Tape recordings preserve the child's words for years!

Students can tape individually or with a buddy.

Tell about your family

Shared Reading

Shared reading is an oral-language and reading activity. See **Chapter 3** for ideas and activities.

Tell, Write, and Read

Add writing and reading to show-and-tell time. As a student shares orally with the class, write a sentence from the student's presentation on a sentence strip. Then show the sentence strip to the class and read the sentence. Have the class reread the sentence aloud. At the end of the day, students who shared that day can take their individual sentence strips home.

Author Presentations

Divide the class into groups of three to five students. Assign or let groups choose a children's author about whom to present an oral report. Have groups gather information and books by the author. Groups then take turns sharing about authors and setting up a tabletop display of books.

Sharing Silent Reading

Take a few minutes at the conclusion of silent-reading time to hold a class discussion about books students are reading. This spreads the word through the class about books students find especially enjoyable.

Individual Retelling

After reading a story or chapter, ask a student to present an oral summary. Check that student's name off a class list. The next time, have another student do the retelling. Continue until everyone has had an opportunity to give an oral summary. A reproducible class list form is on **page 99** in **Chapter 5**.

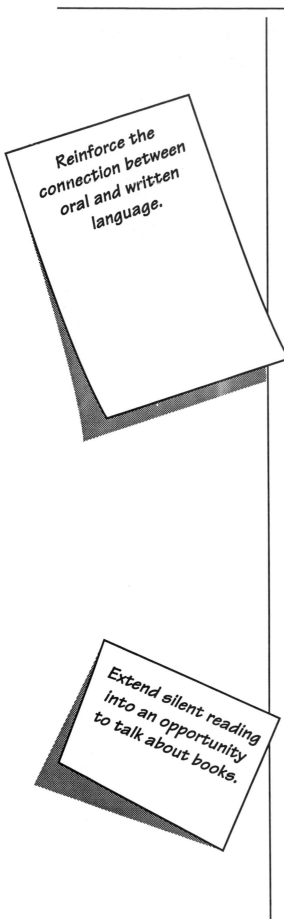

Reinforce the connection between oral and written language.

Extend silent reading into an opportunity to talk about books.

Group Retelling

After your class reads a story or chapter, ask the class how the chapter began. Elicit a sentence from one student about the beginning. Then ask what happened next, and elicit a second sentence from a different student. Continue leading the class through the story in this way.

Reinforce story sequence with retelling activities.

At the beginning, Ned was sad because his dog was lost.

Oral chapter reviews increase comprehension and ensure continuity.

Yesterday's Chapter

This activity complements a chapter book you read aloud or one students read alone. Before reading a chapter, do an oral review of the chapter read the previous day. This refreshes students' memories about the story and reminds them where they left off. Ask students how yesterday's chapter began. Elicit a sentence from one of the students. Then ask what happened next. Have another student provide a sentence.

Continue leading the class through an oral summary of the chapter. Then read the next chapter. This enhances comprehension because it gets everyone "back into the story where they left off" prior to resuming reading. It is also helpful to students who were absent and missed the chapter being discussed.

> *An oral summary helps re-establish the story line.*

Family Homework

This wonderful discussion activity helps build a sense of community in the classroom because students have an opportunity to get to know their teacher as a person.

Tell your class that you want them to ask someone in their family to tell them what it was like when he or she was in third (or your) grade. Then tell the class about your third-grade experiences. Tell students the name of your school, your teacher's name, how you got to school, your favorite subjects, recess activities, and so on. At home, students ask an adult in the family to recount experiences from the same grade. The next day at school, have students share the information they learned with a partner.

> *Involving family members strengthens the home-school bond.*

My students looked forward to family homework. Always begin the activity by sharing about yourself. I learned that many of my students went home and told their families the information I had shared, then asked a family member about the family homework topic.

At conferences, many of my students' families commented that they enjoyed sharing remembrances with their children about their own childhoods. By sharing information about yourself first, students get to know you better as well. Here are more ideas for discussion openers the child can ask an adult at home:

- What did you want to be when you grew up?

- Tell me about your school.

- Tell me about your family.

- Did you have any hobbies?

- Tell me about the place where you lived.

- Tell me about a special childhood memory.

- Tell me what you liked to do for fun.

- Did you have to do chores in your family?

- Did you have any pets?

When the teacher models this activity for the class and discloses information about herself, students feel more comfortable talking and writing about themselves. This has a positive effect on both discussion and writing activities.

> Many adults enjoy the opportunity to tell their children about their own childhoods.

End of the Week Chat

On Fridays, get your class ready to go home five minutes early. Then take time for a chat that brings closure to the end of a busy week at school. Tell students what the best part of the week was for you. Ask students to share their feelings about the week. This ends the week on a positive note and bonds the class together by having them discuss experiences they've shared.

> A class chat is a great way to bring closure to the week and end on a positive note.

Turn-and-Teach

Turn-and-teach is a partner activity in which students share or explain something. For example, after reading and discussing a chapter in literature, have students turn to a partner and describe how the chapter made him feel. Or, have students tell their partners the most important thing they learned after reading an article in a classroom newspaper. The benefits of turn-and-teach are that everyone gets to talk to someone who is listening, and it just takes a few moments.

Weekly Discussion Question

Designate a specific day and time of the week for the "Weekly Discussion Question." After lunch on Fridays might be a good time to do this high-interest activity.

Pose a question to the class that has a "yes" or "no" answer. Write the question on the chalkboard and read it aloud to the class. Then hold a class discussion about the question. Following the discussion, have students "vote" by placing a magnet under "yes" or "no." (Magnets should not have students' names.)

This activity encourages students to think, listen to others' viewpoints, and arrive at a carefully considered answer to the question. You will find that it is easy to come up with a question. Students may suggest topics for this activity. Your students will look forward to this exercise weekly. Here are some ideas to get you started:

- Should parents set children's bedtimes?
- Should parents leave children home alone?
- Should parents control the amount of television their children watch?
- Should there be a law about wearing seat belts?
- Should there be a law requiring bicycle and motorcycle riders to wear helmets?
- Should schools require students to wear uniforms?

Encourage students to share what they've learned with each other.

Class discussions can help students develop tolerance for classmates' opinions and ideas.

Should teachers give homework?

yes | no

Say It With Feeling

Copy sentences of dialog from literature and basal reader stories on cards. Give each student a card to read silently, then practice reading aloud with expression. Have students take turns reading their cards aloud to the class, to a small group, or partners.

Directions for making magnets are on page 165.

Let students practice reading with expression.

"Oh no, here comes that big dog!"

"I miss my grandmother so much. I think about her every day."

"Wow! It's a brand new bicycle. Thanks."

Managing Oral-Language Activities

Many oral-language exercises work best as partner or small-group activities. Consider assigning oral-language groups or sharing partners for the month.

Give students a variety of oral-language experiences.

Set a positive tone for your classroom community.

Oral Language Throughout the Year

Have students do a variety of oral-language activities throughout the year.

1. Speaking from personal experience

- caring for a pet
- a vacation or trip
- your best birthday
- having brothers or sisters
- an unforgettable experience
- something funny that happened

2. Explaining

- how to play a game
- how to make something
- how to clean and organize your desk
- how to brush your teeth
- how to clean your room

3. Interviewing

- a classmate or friend
- the teacher
- a school staff member
- a family member

4. Reporting

- a news event
- an important event at school

5. Presenting a review

- a book
- a movie
- a video game
- tv show
- a place you visited

Lizards are reptiles.
They are
cold-blooded.

6. Sharing expertise

- about an animal
- about a place
- about a person
- about your hobby
- about a sport

7. Dramatizing creatively

- present a puppet show
- act out a scene from a story
- pretend to be a famous person; have listeners guess who you are

Oral-language activities build confidence.

8. Improvising —"What if . . ."

- you missed the school bus
- it snowed in July
- you lost your lunch money
- you found a lost animal

9. Telling about books

Post a chart or give students a copy of "Telling About Books" on **page 142.**

Telling About Books

1. Where and when does the story take place?

2. Who are the main characters?

3. What is one of the main characters like?

4. Who is your favorite character? Why?

5. Which picture in the book do you like best? Why?

6. Which part of the story do you like best?

7. How do you feel about the end of the story?

8. What do you remember most about the story?

9. Do you think others would like to read this book? Why or why not?

10. Would you read another book by this author? Why or why not?

Learning About Literature

reproducible page

NOTES

NOTES

Theme Study

Theme study is a curriculum-wide focus on a topic. Learning activities throughout the classroom day can be linked to the theme study. Theme study is also referred to as the thematic approach, thematic teaching, or thematic units. In my view, there are two kinds of themes: simple and complex.

Simple themes have a narrow focus. Because of the narrow scope, simple themes are usually covered in a shorter time than complex themes. Examples of simple themes include teddy bears, apples, and kites.

Complex themes have a broader scope. Many subtopics can be studied within the theme. A complex theme topic serves as an umbrella with subtopics that naturally fall beneath its broad scope. Complex themes lend themselves to longer periods of study. Examples of complex themes include Native Americans, ecology, families, friendship, and communities.

Themes can be simple (narrow) or complex (broad).

Both simple and complex themes are appropriate in any classroom.

a simple theme

Topic: Apples
- Read Johnny Appleseed
- Write stories in shape books
- Apple Math Activity
- Science
  5 senses - need 12 apples
- Art - Class mural about Johnny Appleseed.

a complex theme

ECOLOGY
Taking Care of Our Earth

Pollution
air
water
ozone layer
solid waste
litter

Food Chain

Saving Energy
home
school
neighborhood
community
recycling

Endangered Species
plants
animals
birds
rain forests

Some educators and authors believe that complex themes are more valuable than simple themes. In my view, it adds interest and variety to use both. I believe your teaching year should include a blend of the two. You can spend weeks or months on a complex-theme study, then spend a few days or a week on a simple topic. Both kinds of themes are meaningful and have a valid place in classrooms at all grade levels.

Rationale

Theme study allows you to link learning activities throughout the day to the theme-study focus, giving students a broader and deeper perspective. The learning day is connected rather than fragmented. When you unify the curriculum with themes, you have opportunities to focus on the theme throughout the learning day.

Gathering and Organizing Materials for Themes

Label a folder or box with the theme topic. Place your lists of ideas and materials about your theme study in the folder. Here are three ways you can organize the ideas and materials in educational magazines:

1. Tear magazines apart and file material according to topics. File a bulletin-board idea about endangered species in your folder for that topic. When you are ready to focus on that topic, your ideas and materials are already collected in the theme/topic folder.

2. If you like to keep your magazines intact, photocopy the ideas and place them in your theme/topic folder. Filing your materials and ideas by topic is a sound organizational strategy.

3. Create an index for your educational magazines. It takes just minutes to create this index in a file folder. Label a file folder with the title of the magazine. Then photocopy the table of contents from each issue. Staple the tables of contents in chronological sequence in the folder. When you need to locate ideas about endangered species you can flip through your index to determine which issue contains the material you are looking for. It is faster to look through the index than searching through the actual magazines. Each time you receive another issue of the magazine, photocopy the table of contents and add it to your index.

Don't forget the great materials found in magazines. Create an index and check it often.

SCHOOLDAYS INDEX

Kim M.

file folder front

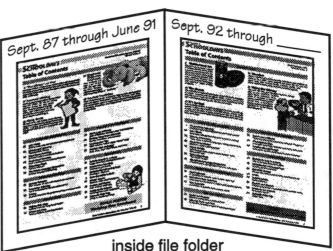

Sept. 87 through June 91

Sept. 92 through _____

inside file folder

Teachers Helping Teachers

Tell colleagues about your theme-study topic. Perhaps they have some ideas to share. Jot down ideas you gather and add them to your theme folder.

Do grade-level planning with other teachers. Meet with colleagues to discuss themes studied at your grade level. Let each teacher take responsibility for organizing and planning certain theme topics for her grade level. Then share plans with all teachers on that grade level. Teachers can adapt and change the basic plans to suit their individual classes. Coordinating plans with other teachers saves time and work!

Working with other teachers saves time and work—everyone benefits!

Share teaching materials to save time and money. If all three second-grade classrooms do a theme study about ecology, label a box "Ecology—Second Grade." If each class focuses on ecology at different times during the year, teachers can take turns using the materials in the box. The box could contain a variety of ecology-related materials such as charts, big books, a classroom set of paperback books, bulletin-board materials, and so on.

Link Literature to Theme Study

There are many wonderful resource books for teachers that list works of literature by topic. Books are also listed by authors and titles. Ask the children's librarian at the public library about these and other useful references:

A to Zoo—Subject Access to Children's Picture Books

Children's Books in Print by Lima and Lima

These books are updated annually and provide lists of literature by titles, authors, and subjects.

Theme-Study Planning

Many teachers spend hours developing detailed, extensive plans for themes. Often they find there isn't enough time to carry out all the activities, or they feel rushed trying to fit everything into the learning day. Instead, do a limited amount of planning ahead of time so your theme study can be more flexible and follows the interests of the class.

Take a look at the Theme-Study Planning Forms on **pages 150–152**. Place copies of these handy reproducible forms in your theme folders. Use them to keep track of the activities you implement throughout your theme study. The forms can save you time and work in the future when you repeat a theme study with another class.

Use the forms to jot down a few ideas you plan to use at the start of the theme study. Then continue to add ideas to the planning sheets as you actually go through the theme. After completing a theme study, write down things you want to do differently in the future. Make a note of how much class time was required for various activities. This information will be helpful when you want to focus on the theme another year with another class.

Planning sheets save time and help you be more flexible.

Theme Study Plans - page 1

Topic

Reading

Ten Steps for Themes
1. Family Letter ✓
2. Vocabulary Cluster
3. Access Prior Knowledge
4. Questions
5. Theme Table/Bulletin Board
6. Theme Folders
7. Theme Journals
8. Reading Aloud
9. Learn

Writing

FS-8128 *100% Practical*   reproducible page
150

Theme Study Plans - page 3

Topic

Art/Music/ Games

Theme Study Plans - page 2

Topic

Social Studies

Science

© Frank Schaffer Publications, Inc.   reproducible page
151   FS-8128 *100% Practical*

Theme Study Plans - page 1

Topic

Reading

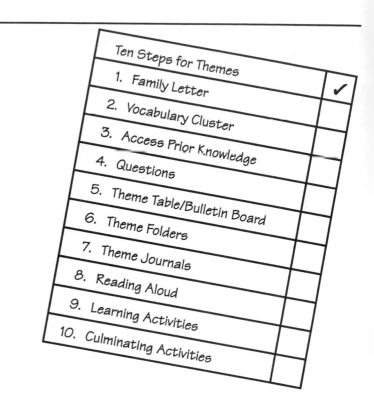

Ten Steps for Themes	
1. Family Letter	✓
2. Vocabulary Cluster	
3. Access Prior Knowledge	
4. Questions	
5. Theme Table/Bulletin Board	
6. Theme Folders	
7. Theme Journals	
8. Reading Aloud	
9. Learning Activities	
10. Culminating Activities	

Writing

FS-8128 *100% Practical*

© Frank Schaffer Publications, Inc.

Theme Study Plans - page 2

Topic

Social Studies

Science

Topic

Art/Music/Games

Other (Field Trips, Resource Speakers, Videos)

Culminating Activities

Implementing Theme Studies

Effective teachers have always integrated and correlated their instructional programs. My goal is to provide an array of specific activities to make theme studies meaningful to students. You can choose activities that fit your students, your teaching style, and the particular theme you've chosen. Be certain to offer a balance of activities for

- your whole class
- small groups
- partners
- individual students

> Balance the learning day with activities for groups and individuals.

A 10-Step Plan for Theme Studies

Step 1: Inform Parents

Use the reproducible parent letter on the following page to inform parents of your theme study. Encourage parents to support their children's learning about the topic. As a bonus, you may discover parents who can contribute information or resources to the theme study.

> When parents know about your theme focus, they can engage in "school talk" with their children.

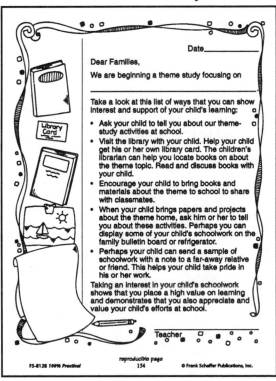

Date_____

Dear Families,

We are beginning a theme study focusing on

_____

Take a look at this list of ways that you can show interest and support of your child's learning:

- Ask your child to tell you about our theme-study activities at school.

- Visit the library with your child. Help your child get his or her own library card. The children's librarian can help you locate books on about the theme topic. Read and discuss books with your child.

- Encourage your child to bring books and materials about the theme to school to share with classmates.

- When your child brings papers and projects about the theme home, ask him or her to tell you about these activities. Perhaps you can display some of your child's schoolwork on the family bulletin board or refrigerator.

- Perhaps your child can send a sample of schoolwork with a note to a far-away relative or friend. This helps your child take pride in his or her work.

Taking an interest in your child's schoolwork shows that you place a high value on learning and demonstrates that you also appreciate and value your child's efforts at school.

Teacher _____

Step 2: Start a Vocabulary Cluster

Display a large piece of chart paper labeled with your theme topic. Announce the theme to the class and brainstorm together to come up with a list of words about the theme. Ask your students for suggestions and jot them on the word chart. Tell students to watch for additional theme-related vocabulary words to add to the chart. Continue to add words to the chart as they come up during the theme study. The word chart can then be used for different activities such as these:

- a spelling reference for students
- words for writing activities
- vocabulary games
- classification activities
- making picture dictionaries
- ideas for writing activities

Since the word list comes from the students, it will be different each time you teach the theme. Be sure to let each new group develop its own word list.

Step 3: Access Prior Knowledge

Hold a class discussion on what your students already know about the theme topic. This discussion helps the class focus on the theme topic. It also helps students connect what they already know with what they are about to learn.

Rather than assign predetermined vocabulary lists, let students develop their own.

Find out what your students already know about the subject.

I went to the White House once!

Step 4: Establish a Purpose for Learning

Ask students what questions they might have about the theme topic. What do your students want to find out about the topic? If the theme study is about rain forests, you might prompt the discussion by saying, "I've been wondering if there are any rain forests in the United States. Have you ever thought about that?" The purpose of this activity is to draw students into the topic. Following this discussion, most students will have a question or two they hope to have answered through the theme study. This activity helps students set a purpose for learning.

Find out what else they would like to know about the subject.

Step 5: Set Up a Theme Table and/or Bulletin Board

Encourage students to bring books, news clippings, and objects that pertain to the theme. These items can be shared and displayed.

Step 6: Theme Folders

Folders help students keep track of papers and materials that go with themes. Provide a theme folder for each student. Students can decorate folder covers. Materials tend to get lost or damaged in desks. I recommend establishing a box or basket in which to store theme folders. Take a look at the ideas for making folders on the following page.

Have each student keep a theme folder or portfolio.

How to Make Folders

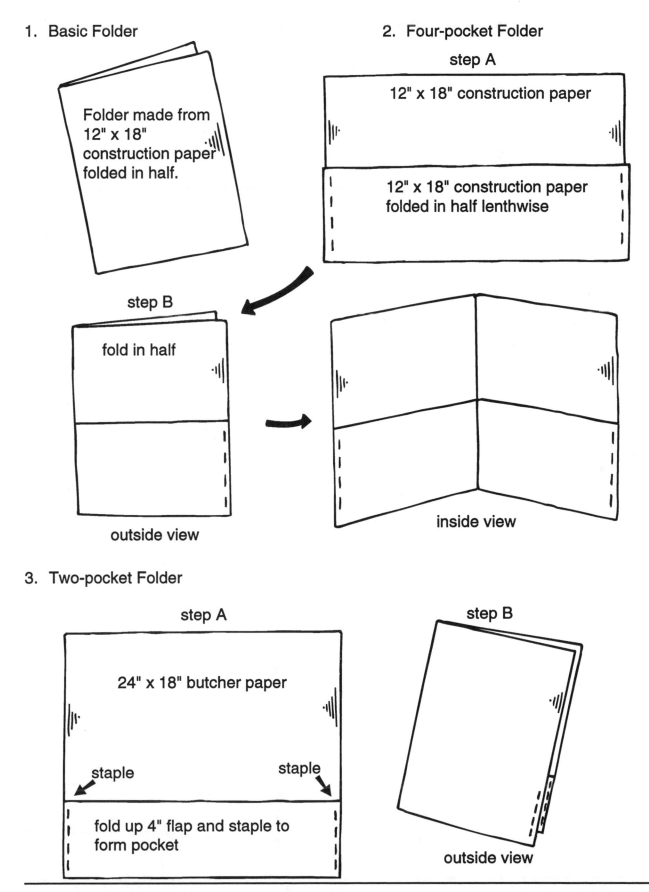

1. Basic Folder

Folder made from 12" x 18" construction paper folded in half.

2. Four-pocket Folder

step A

12" x 18" construction paper

12" x 18" construction paper folded in half lenthwise

step B

fold in half

outside view

inside view

3. Two-pocket Folder

step A

24" x 18" butcher paper

staple

staple

fold up 4" flap and staple to form pocket

step B

outside view

Step 7: Theme Journals

Link writing to your theme studies through note-books and journals. In kindergarten or first grade the teacher can keep the theme journal on the chalkboard or chart paper. At the end of each day, elicit a few sentences from students about the theme. Jot the date and print the sentences on chart paper. Use the journal entry for a shared-reading activity. Read the sentences aloud, tracking the print from left to right with a pointer or fingertip as you read. Then ask your class to reread the journal entry aloud with you.

Link learning with notebooks and journals.

A group journal is perfect for grades K–1.

Individual journals help students organize information.

<u>Learning About Bears</u>

November 2
Bears are mammals. Their cubs are born alive. They drink milk from their mothers.

chart

In grades 2–6, students can write journal entries in individual theme journals. Students may write questions about the topic or about something new they learned. They could also keep a separate journal for the theme or use a separate section of a binder or notebook.

My Oceanography Journal

Andrew M.

Double-entry journals work well with theme studies. Students write journal entries on the right-hand page and use the left hand page for questions, lists of ideas, and illustrations.

See **Chapter 5** "Your Writing Program," **pages 87-90,** for more ideas about journals.

> Double-entry journals are ideal for theme studies.

Step 8: Reading Aloud

Select a book to read aloud that correlates with your theme study. See **Chapter 2** for a wealth of strategies to add value to reading aloud.

> Reading aloud adds dimension to any theme study.

Step 9: Theme Study Activities

In **Chapter 11**, "Learning Activities and Projects," you'll find a gold mine of ideas for whole-class, small-group and individual activities that can be used with theme study.

Step 10: Culminating Activities

Wrap up your theme study with a special culminating activity or project. Here are just two ideas:

Theme Presentation—This presentation idea is fun, easy to implement, and involves every student. To prepare, hold a class discussion about information and projects the class might want to share about the theme. Then assign each student a part in the presentation. For example, one student can be the greeter who welcomes the visitors to your class. Another student can show and explain a graph, and several students might hold up books that were published by cooperative learning groups about the theme. Have each student jot a reminder of what he is supposed to do and say during the presentation.

> Wrap up your theme with a special presentation.

Students can present in pairs or groups!

It's also a good idea to have students write the name of the person whom they are to follow in the presentation on the card. Invite other classes, parents, staff members, and guests to your classroom for the presentation. When visitors arrive, students assume their positions for the presentation. Students can refer to their cards if they forget what to say or whom they follow.

One of the best features of this type of presentation is that students can carry it out successfully on their own. The teacher can step back and enjoy watching students share what they've learned.

Students love to make books connected to themes.

Classroom Publishing About Themes—Writing a book about a theme helps students compile and synthesize what they have learned. Students can write individual books or class books. Take a look at the classroom-publishing ideas in **Chapter 6**. For example, wrap up a theme study in K–1 grades by making a class book as described on **pages 105–106**. In grades 2–6, have the group write a class non-fiction book using cooperative-learning groups as described on **page 112**.

Enrich your students' learning often with themes. Whether simple or complex, students will enjoy and benefit from a variety of theme studies.

NOTES

NOTES

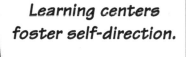

Good news—centers do not have to take a lot of teacher-development time!

Learning Centers— Simple and Effective

Learning centers can be used in a variety of ways in your classroom. They do not have to be elaborate, decorative productions that teachers spend hours putting together. After reading this chapter, you will have ideas and techniques that can help you implement centers effectively in your classroom. My learning-center ideas are easy to implement and classroom-tested.

How Learning Centers Benefit Students

Learning centers foster self-direction.

Learning centers give students opportunities to develop a variety of skills including:

- self direction
- decision making
- working independently
- working with others
- sense of responsibility

How Learning Centers Benefit Teachers

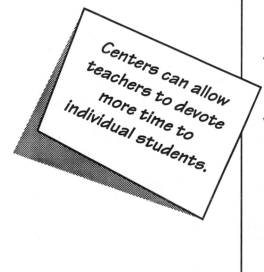

Centers can allow teachers to devote more time to individual students.

Teachers benefit from learning centers in these ways:

- Centers can provide activities for capable students who finish first and say "I'm done."
- When students are self-directed in learning-center activities, the teacher has an opportunity to confer with individual students or small groups.

My Beliefs About Learning Centers

- There are many valid, successful ways to use centers.

- Centers should be easy for teachers to establish, maintain, change, and evaluate.

- All students should have an opportunity to use learning centers. Learning centers should not be used exclusively as rewards for just a few students.

- Center activities can provide practice, enrichment, and extension of the classroom curriculum.

- Teachers need a simple, organized method of record-keeping.

> Centers have to be easy to prepare, use, and track.

Physical Set-Up of Centers

Classrooms are crowded places. Learning centers do not have to take a lot of space in the classroom. Centers where students actually work at the center location are only one type of set-up. You can also have centers where students simply get directions and materials. Students then work on the activities at their own desks. Following are examples of each type.

> Centers need not take up precious classroom space.

Listen-and-Learn Center
Students work at the center.

WORKSHEETS

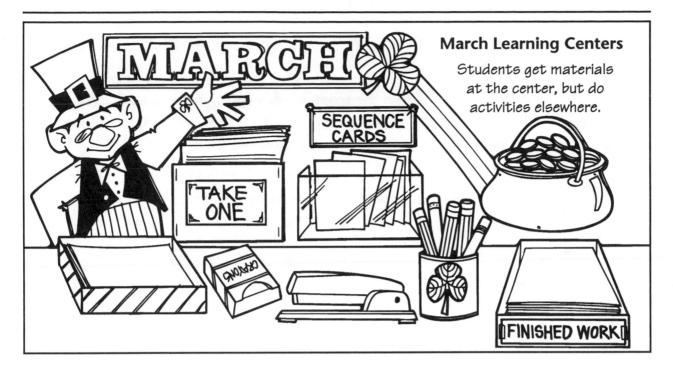

March Learning Centers

Students get materials at the center, but do activities elsewhere.

Grouping Students

Students can work on learning centers in groups, pairs, or individually. Centers could be used during a specific time of day set by the teacher or at the student's discretion. Learning-center groups can be written on the chalkboard.

(chalkboard)	
#4	#5
Sally	Jay
Ben	Brenda
Kyle	Sara
Dina	Heather
Mike	Steven

Magnets make grouping fast and flexible.

Another method is to assign students into groups using magnets with students' names. To make inexpensive magnets that last all year, laminate a piece of 12" x 18" construction paper on both sides. Trace and cut out a circle for each student plus a few extras for new students. Print each student's name on a circle and affix a small piece of adhesive magnetic strip on the back. If your chalkboards are not magnetic, use a metal automotive drip pan or a large cookie sheet.

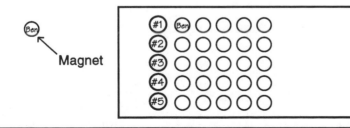

Ben ← Magnet

#1 Ben ○ ○ ○ ○
#2 ○ ○ ○ ○ ○
#3 ○ ○ ○ ○ ○
#4 ○ ○ ○ ○ ○
#5 ○ ○ ○ ○ ○

Content of Learning Centers

Learning centers can provide activities that are within the scope of the regular curriculum, such as practice and review. Centers can also focus on topics and materials that enrich and extend the curriculum.

You already have everything you need in your classroom to create high-interest learning centers. You probably have some learning materials, such as task cards, that you haven't had time to use. Perhaps they can be used through learning centers. You can incorporate regular classroom activities into learning centers.

Make the most of materials you already have on hand.

Ways to Incorporate Learning Centers Into Your Instructional Program

Here are a few successful ways to incorporate learning centers into your instructional program:

- Learning-Center Day—Choose a subject and a day of the week for learning centers. For example, Friday could be "centers day" during math period. You could establish four centers and four groups. Groups go to a different center each Friday. At the end of four weeks students have used all four centers. The teacher only has to change centers every four weeks.

- Learning-Center Week—During a theme study, have students spend one week doing a five-day rotation through five centers that pertain to the theme study.

- Monthly Enrichment Centers—Set up a few enrichment centers at the beginning of each month. Change the centers monthly.

Enrich and extend curriculum through centers.

- Permanent Centers—Wait until the school term is going smoothly and students are accustomed to the flow of the learning day in your classroom. Introduce one permanent center at a time. Explain the concept to the class and tell students that the center will be available all year long. The following month, introduce a second permanent center. Continue to do this until you have several centers established in your classroom.

- Assigned Learning Centers—Learning centers can be a part of your regular instructional program. Select certain activities from your existing program that lend themselves to centers.

Once established, permanent centers are easy to maintain.

Classroom Management Tips

1. Take your time establishing learning centers in your classroom. Students need time to learn how to use centers and do record keeping.

2. Use symbols to make centers easy to use.

   (T)   = Teacher

   (T)___ = Teacher must initial here

   (★)   = Required activity

   (☺)(☺) = Work with a partner

3. Consider having students make a learning center folder. They file record-keeping forms and learning-center activities for the week in the folder. Have the class store folders in a box rather than in individual desks. Look at the ideas for work folders for students on **page 157** in **Chapter 8**.

4. At the end of the week, students can take record-keeping forms home. Pencil and paper activities can be stapled to the form.

Symbols are quick and easy to use.

> *The key to successful center time is clear expectations and follow-through.*

5. You can have an envelope or box for finished work at the learning center.

6. When you begin using centers, state your expectations about behavior and have groups go to their centers one at a time. Hold a class problem-solving discussion to evaluate work habits, behavior, and any problems that may have occurred during learning-center time.

7. The first few times students use centers, practice record keeping together as a group. Do record keeping after working in centers.

8. To save time and work, make some of your centers permanent. See the examples of permanent centers on **pages 176–185, 188**. You do not have to spend time changing the centers or teaching students how to use permanent centers once they have been introduced.

9. In most classrooms there are a few students who are irresponsible. Check with those students frequently to verify progress.

Ways to Use Learning Centers

There are many ways to use centers effectively. You could be using centers one way during language time and differently in connection with science or math. Take a look at the advantages and disadvantages of the learning-center methods described in this chapter. Consider these options:

> *Use different types of centers for different purposes.*

- five-day rotation

- five-week rotation

- enrichment centers

- combination of assigned and enrichment centers

Five-Day Rotation

Establish five learning center activities for the week. Assign students into five groups. By the end of the week, all students have rotated through all five centers.

Center activities should be designed for independent work. If one center requires direction, the teacher can work at that center each day while groups function independently at the other four centers. Introduce and briefly explain all five centers to the whole class on Monday. The steps for implementing five-day rotation:

1. Plan and establish five centers.
2. Divide students into five groups.
3. Decide on a time of day for learning centers.
4. Show students their group assignments on the chalkboard as shown on **page 165**.
5. On Monday, introduce all five centers to the whole class.
6. Give students a record-keeping form.

Have groups go to a different center each day. After completing the activity at the center, students track their progress on their record-keeping forms. Look at the record-keeping ideas beginning on **page 173**.

> Once directions are given, students should be able to use centers independently.

(Specific checklist)

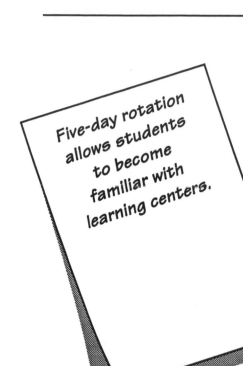

Five-day rotation allows students to become familiar with learning centers.

Advantages of Five-Day Rotation:

- You can establish a specific learning-center period.

- Students become familiar with using learning centers.

- Students learn to do record-keeping.

- All students use all five centers.

- The teacher can establish one center that requires direction where he or she works with students while other students work at four different centers independently.

Disadvantages of Five-Day Rotation:

- At the week's end, all students have done all five activities. The net result is no different than if the whole class did a different activity together each day of the week.

Five-Week Rotation

This is similar to the five-day rotation described, except that groups work at a different center each week. At the end of five weeks, groups have completed all five centers.

Enrichment Centers for Capable Students

Enrichment centers are for capable, efficient students who have extra time to do work above and beyond required class assignments. These centers are used when students have extra time, so you do not need to establish a limited learning-center time period. Take the following steps to implement enrichment centers.

Enrichment centers can meet the needs of capable students.

1. Plan and establish enrichment-center activities. Explain each center to one student in your class who is likely to have time to use enrichment centers. That student can be the "student teacher" for that center. Post the name of the student teacher at the center.

2. Explain that centers can only be used by students who have finished all required work.

3. Avoid making enrichment centers that need to be changed frequently. Take a look at the specific center ideas on **pages 176–188**.

Let a capable student teach others to use a center.

Advantages of Enrichment Centers:

• Activities are ready and available for students who finish required work and have extra time.

• You can make these center activities more challenging since students who use them are the most capable students in your class.

Disadvantages of Enrichment Centers:

• Students who have difficulty completing classwork never have an opportunity to use these enrichment centers.

"World Geography Challenge"

Folders

FINISHED WORK

> *A combination of required and enrichment centers may best meet the needs of all students.*

Required centers can be prescriptive.

Combination Assigned and Enrichment Centers

I think this is the most effective way to use learning centers at all grade levels. All students are required to complete certain learning-center activities. Upon completion of required activities, students may choose other learning-center activities. Follow these steps to implement combination assigned/enrichment centers.

1. Plan and establish centers.

2. Designate which centers are required by marking them with a ★.

3. Decide if you want students to use the required centers in a specific order. I recommend encouraging students to do required centers in any sequence. If required centers can be done in random order, students will be dispersed across the activities. Your entire class will not be trying to do the same center at the same time.

4. Create a record-keeping form.

5. Explain required centers to the class at the beginning of the week.

6. Explain enrichment centers to the class at midweek.

Advantages of Combination Centers:

- All students get to use center activities.

- The teacher sets a minimum number of centers that are required activities. Set this number realistically so that all students can complete required centers. Then most students will have time to choose at least one more learning center.

- You can make your learning centers prescriptive. At the beginning of the week, indicate which activities you want each student to do on his or her checklist. You can require students to complete activities that will be most beneficial to them.

- If you have students who are pulled out for special programs and therefore have less time than others to work on learning centers, you can assign those students fewer required activities so they can successfully complete them.

Checklists and contracts motivate students and help them track their own progress.

Record-Keeping Ideas for Centers

Checklists or contracts can be especially useful with learning centers. They offer these advantages:

- they motivate students
- they help students be organized
- they keep students focused and on task
- they can be used for recording progress

Record-Keeping Forms—Provide each student with a record-keeping form on which to record his or her progress. These forms can be taken home at the end of the week or month. This is an easy way to inform parents of center activities in your classroom.

You can make a checklist that students take home at the end of the week. If you have five centers each week, you could use either of the checklists shown here. The generic checklist saves time because the teacher does not have to create a new checklist for each new week of center activities. Simply have students copy center activities from the chalkboard onto the generic checklist format. You could have students do this at the beginning of the week when you introduce the centers.

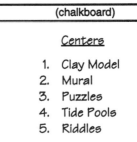

(chalkboard)

Centers

1. Clay Model
2. Mural
3. Puzzles
4. Tide Pools
5. Riddles

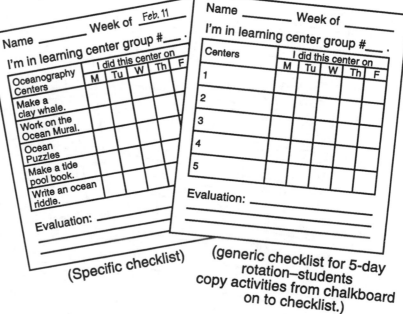

(Specific checklist)

(generic checklist for 5-day rotation—students copy activities from chalkboard on to checklist.)

> Save time by rotating specific content within a pre-programmed set of centers.

Programmed Checklists or Contracts—If you have 12 centers, as shown on **pages 186–187**, you can use either checklist shown below. I prefer Example B because it is not specific. You can reproduce the same checklist week after week. The activities change but the programmed checklist does not. Students become familiar with the format, and parents appreciate receiving a weekly report.

This is the way I managed combination required and enrichment learning centers in my classroom. On Mondays, I gave students a new checklist to keep in their work folders. Required activities had to be done by Thursday when I collected students' folders. On Thursdays I jotted a comment on each student's checklist. Paper and pencil activities were stapled to the checklist. Often students who had been absent during the week were able to finish required activities on Fridays. Students took checklists home on Fridays to share with their families.

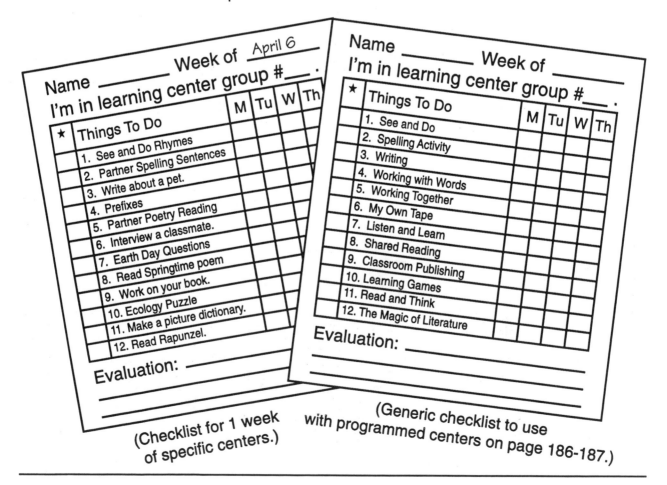

Name _____ Week of __April 6__
I'm in learning center group #___.

★ Things To Do	M	Tu	W	Th
1. See and Do Rhymes				
2. Partner Spelling Sentences				
3. Write about a pet.				
4. Prefixes				
5. Partner Poetry Reading				
6. Interview a classmate.				
7. Earth Day Questions				
8. Read Springtime poem				
9. Work on your book.				
10. Ecology Puzzle				
11. Make a picture dictionary.				
12. Read Rapunzel.				

Evaluation: _____

(Checklist for 1 week of specific centers.)

Name _____ Week of _____
I'm in learning center group #___.

★ Things To Do	M	Tu	W	Th
1. See and Do				
2. Spelling Activity				
3. Writing				
4. Working with Words				
5. Working Together				
6. My Own Tape				
7. Listen and Learn				
8. Shared Reading				
9. Classroom Publishing				
10. Learning Games				
11. Read and Think				
12. The Magic of Literature				

Evaluation: _____

(Generic checklist to use with programmed centers on page 186-187.)

Puzzle Formats—This is a highly motivating and effective way to keep students on track and to record their progress in learning centers.

Use a reproducible puzzle format and have students color sections as they complete activities. Some teachers make a new format or checklist each week. You can save time and work by making a generic format. Instead of writing specific activities on the puzzle, write them on the chalkboard. The following week, you can reuse the generic puzzle format and simply change specific center activities on the chalkboard, making activity #1 a different phonics activity. Take a look at the examples below.

Puzzle record-keeping forms are especially motivating.

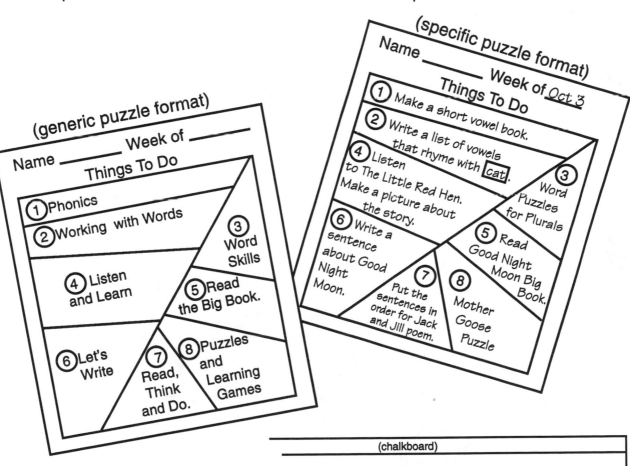

(chalkboard)

1. Make a short vowel book.
2. Make a list of words that rhyme with cat .
3. Word puzzles for plurals.
4. Listen to The Little Red Hen. Make a picture about the story.
5. Read Good Night Moon Big Book.
6. Write a sentence about Good Night Moon.
7. Put the sentences in order for Jack and Jill poem.
8. Mother Goose Puzzle

Students read specific activities from chalkboard.

Learning centers are a great way to foster independence and responsibility.

Examples of Learning Centers

Perhaps the centers shown on the next few pages will provide useful ideas for centers and/or management techniques. Centers can add high-interest activities to your classroom. And they can give students opportunities for assuming responsibility and making choices. Look at **page 133** and **pages 140-142** in **Chapter 7** for Ideas.

Tape Center or Listening Center - use all year

Students work **at** this center.

(directions for tape recorder)

Listen and Learn

1. Put in the tape
2. Put on
3. Push
4. When the tape stops, push
5. Put the tape back.

(directions for my own tape)

My Own Tape

1. Put in your tape.
2. Push ___ ___ to record.
3. Say "Today is _____."

Read aloud into your tape.

← Clip new activity here each week.

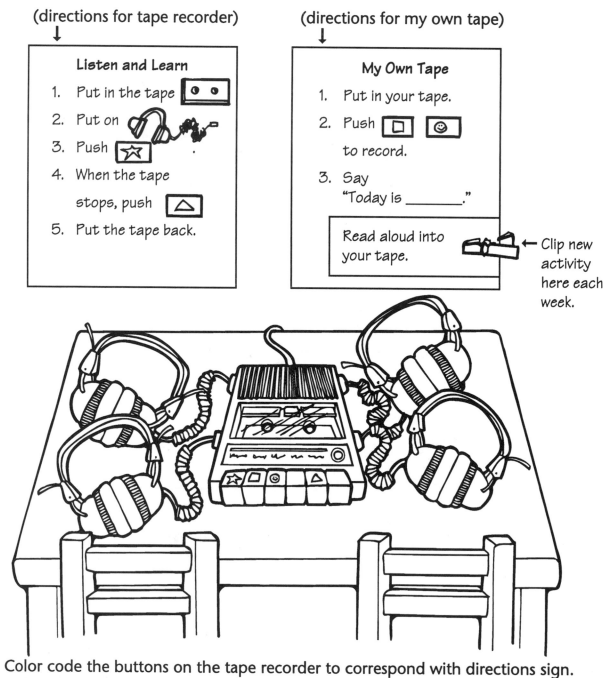

Color code the buttons on the tape recorder to correspond with directions sign.

Learning About the U.S.A. - use all year

Students get folder at the center, then work elsewhere.

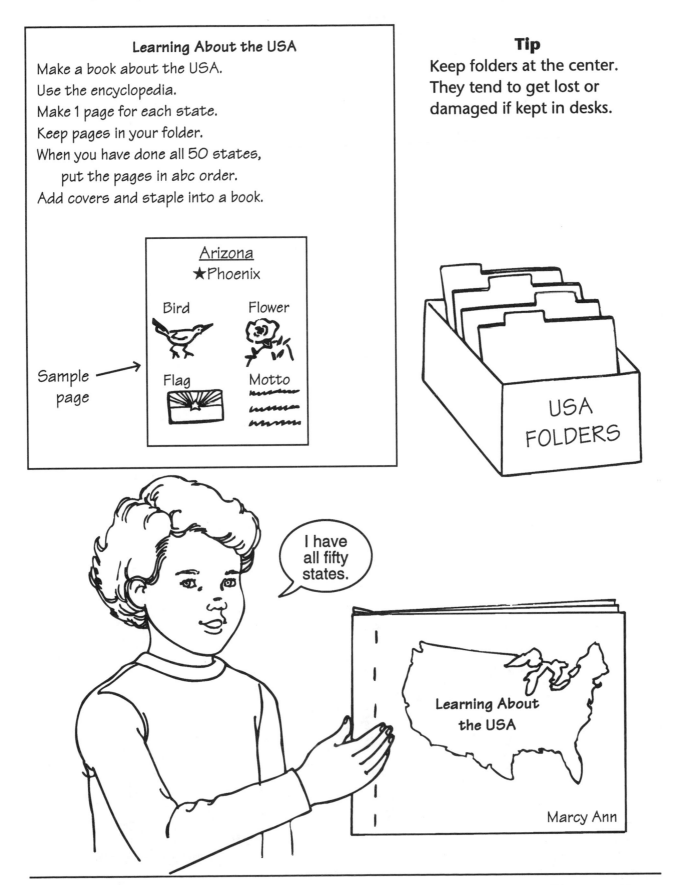

Learning About the USA

Make a book about the USA.

Use the encyclopedia.

Make 1 page for each state.

Keep pages in your folder.

When you have done all 50 states,
   put the pages in abc order.

Add covers and staple into a book.

Sample page →

Arizona
★Phoenix

Bird   Flower

Flag   Motto

Tip

Keep folders at the center.
They tend to get lost or
damaged if kept in desks.

USA FOLDERS

I have all fifty states.

Learning About the USA

Marcy Ann

The World of Living Things - use all year

Students get folder at the center, then work elsewhere.

The World of Living Things

Make a book about the animals, birds, fish, insects, reptiles, amphibians, ...
Use the encyclopedia.
Make 1 page for each living thing.
Keep pages in your folder.
At the end of the year, you can make a book.

Canary

Sample page

Colorful picture

3 facts about the living thing

I made sections in my book for each classification of living things.

My Book About Living Things

Ryan

Get the Facts About the USA - use task cards for this center

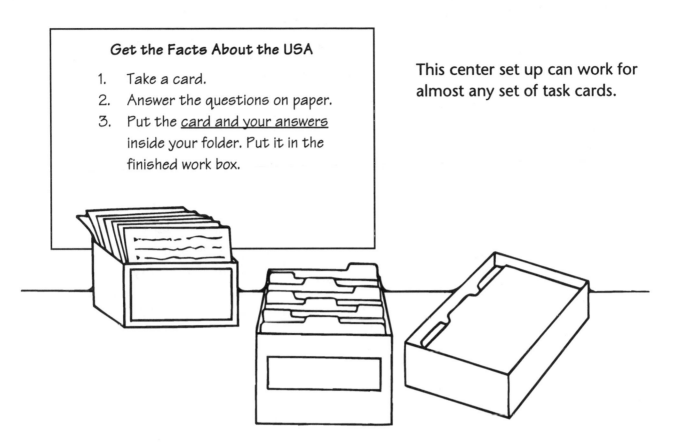

Get the Facts About the USA

1. Take a card.
2. Answer the questions on paper.
3. Put the <u>card and your answers</u> inside your folder. Put it in the finished work box.

This center set up can work for almost any set of task cards.

Inside Student's folder
When a student has checked off on a card, the teacher can ✓ off or initial that state. Students can look in their folders to see which states still need to be done.

Tip: Perhaps a parent who has offered to help at home could mark students' answer sheets. Send folders home every Friday with an answer key. Show the helper how to ✓ students off in their folders.

Monthly Learning Activities - use center all year
Post new activity list and make new folders for each month.

Students get folder at the center, then work elsewhere.

March

* 1. Make a picture of yourself flying a kite on a windy day.
*2. Write a haiku poem about spring.
*3. Write 10 spelling words on shamrocks. Paste them in abc order.
*4. Draw an animal you think is interesting. Write 3 facts about the animal.
*5. Draw a rainbow. Look at our science book to make sure you use the correct colors.
*6. Write a note to your family about your feelings about the fourth grade.
 7. "March comes in like a lion and goes out like a lamb." Copy this saying and write to explain what it means.
 8. Read a riddle book. Copy 1 riddle, Illustrate the riddle.
 9. Trace your handprint. Write words to describe yourself on each finger.
10. Draw a picture and write a rule about bicycle safety.

*Required Activities

At the begining of the month, have each student make a folder with ten pages.
Students do activity #1 on page 1.
Students take the folder home at the end of the month.

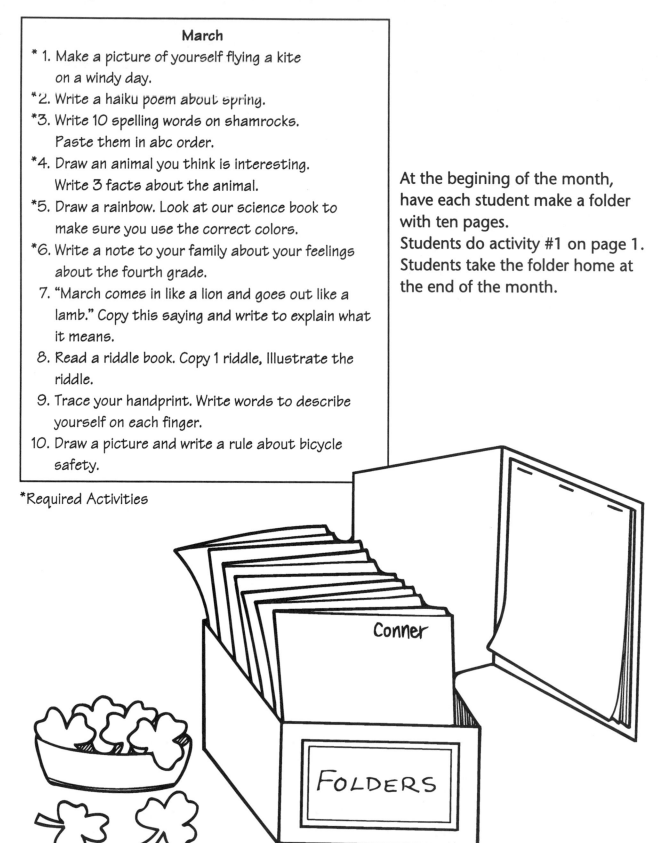

The Magic of Literature - use all year

Students get folder at the center, then work elsewhere.

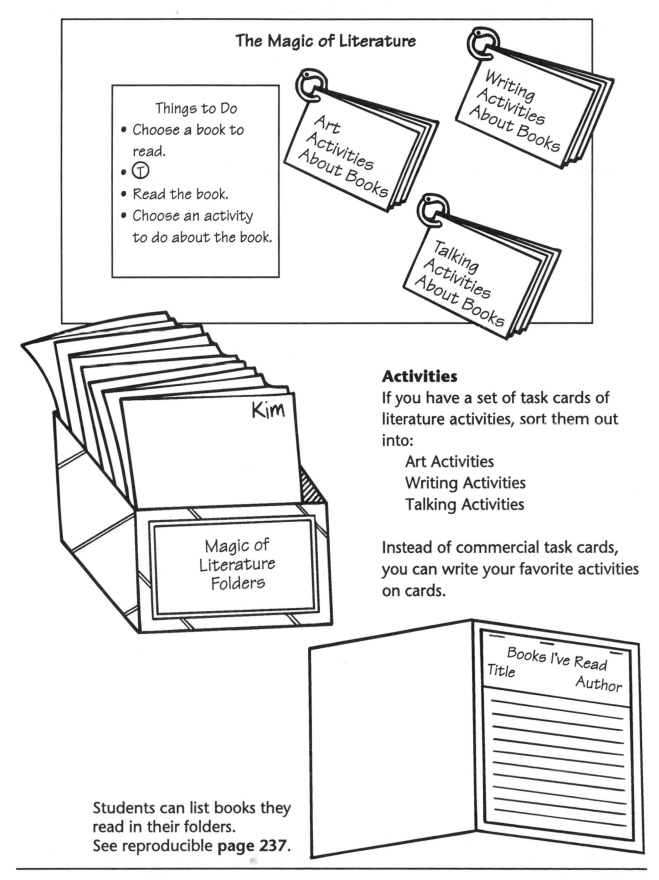

The Magic of Literature

Things to Do
- Choose a book to read.
- ⓣ
- Read the book.
- Choose an activity to do about the book.

Art Activities About Books

Writing Activities About Books

Talking Activities About Books

Kim

Magic of Literature Folders

Activities

If you have a set of task cards of literature activities, sort them out into:

Art Activities
Writing Activities
Talking Activities

Instead of commercial task cards, you can write your favorite activities on cards.

Books I've Read
Title   Author

Students can list books they read in their folders.
See reproducible **page 237**.

Encyclopedia Quiz Center - use all year

Students get folder and materials at the center, then work elsewhere.

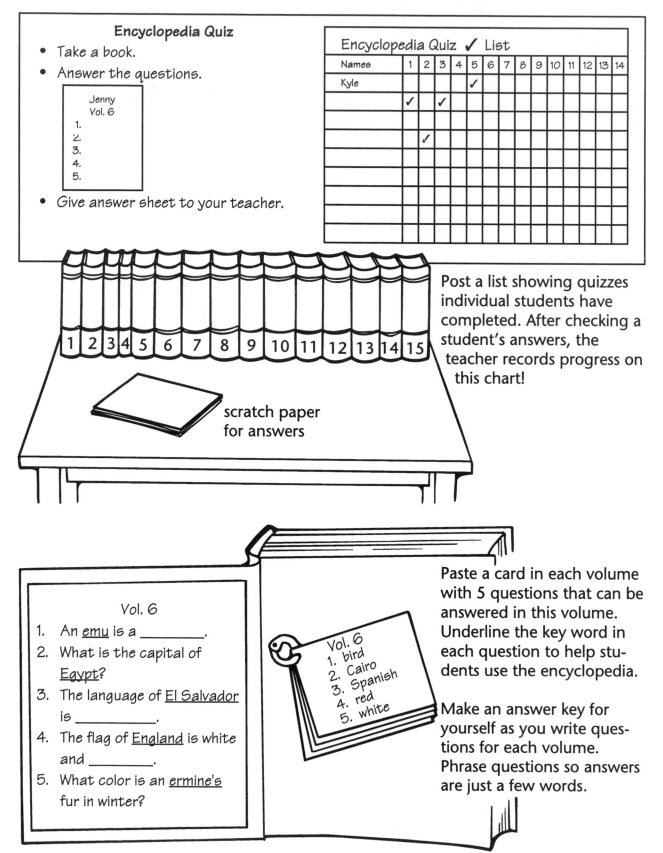

Encyclopedia Quiz

- Take a book.
- Answer the questions.

  Jenny
  Vol. 6
  1.
  2.
  3.
  4.
  5.

- Give answer sheet to your teacher.

Encyclopedia Quiz ✓ List													
Names	1	2	3	4	5	6	7	8	9	10	11	12	13	14
Kyle					✓									
	✓		✓											
		✓												

1 2 3 4 5 6 7 8 9 10 11 12 13 14 15

scratch paper for answers

Post a list showing quizzes individual students have completed. After checking a student's answers, the teacher records progress on this chart!

Vol. 6
1. An <u>emu</u> is a _____ .
2. What is the capital of <u>Egypt</u>?
3. The language of <u>El Salvador</u> is _____ .
4. The flag of <u>England</u> is white and _____ .
5. What color is an <u>ermine's</u> fur in winter?

Vol. 6
1. bird
2. Cairo
3. Spanish
4. red
5. white

Paste a card in each volume with 5 questions that can be answered in this volume. Underline the key word in each question to help students use the encyclopedia.

Make an answer key for yourself as you write questions for each volume. Phrase questions so answers are just a few words.

Tip Have students do volumes in any sequence so everyone isn't waiting for Vol. 1.

See and Do Center - use all year, change activity weekly

(chalkboard)

See and Do		

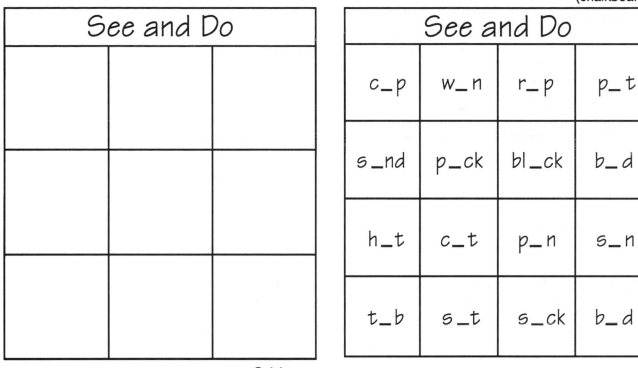

See and Do			
c_p	w_n	r_p	p_t
s_nd	p_ck	bl_ck	b_d
h_t	c_t	p_n	s_n
t_b	s_t	s_ck	b_d

Grid on
chalkboard

The teacher writes activity on the grid. Students do activity
on answer form. This example shows a short-vowel activity.
Students add a vowel to make a real word.
Change skill/activity weekly.

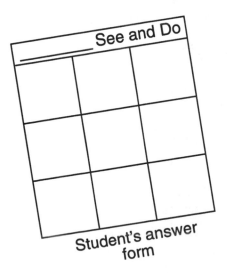

See and Do

Student's answer
form

Emily	See and Do		
cup	win	rip	pot
sand	pick	block	bed
hat	cat	pan	sun
tub	set	sick	bud

Student's completed
answer form

A list of activities for See and Do is on **pages 184** and **185**.

See and Do Activity Ideas

Ideas for See and Do Center on **page 183.**

Teacher writes	**Student**
color words ————————————	colors square that color
red	▓▓▓
singular words ————————————	writes plural
hat	hats
root words ————————————	adds prefixes
view	review
multiplication problems —————	writes products
6 x 6	36
addition problems —————————	writes sums
6 + 4	10
subtraction problems —————————	writes differences
11 - 4	7
number order sequences —————	writes next numbers
12, ____	13
rhyming words ————————————	writes rhyming words
gold	fold
words with synonyms —————————	writes synonyms
big	large
words with antonyms —————————	writes antonyms
hot	cold
phonemes minus initial consonants —	adds an initial consonant to make actual words
__ et	met
phonemes minus final consonants —	adds a final consonant to make actual words
sa __	sad
states ————————————————	writes the capitals
Texas	Austin
animal names ————————————	gives names of baby animals
cow	calf

Adapting See and Do for Different Levels

You can make a grid (on chalkboard and answer form) simple or complex. In first grade, I began with a 9-square grid. Later I changed to 16 squares. In intermediate grades I used 36 squares. You can adapt the grid to meet a variety of levels by simply adjusting the number of squares.

Grid on Chalkboard

See and Do

blue	red	yellow
black	pink	orange
purple	white	brown

See and Do

blue	red	yellow
black	pink	orange
purple	white	brown

Student's answer form

Grid on Chalkboard

See and Do

64	36	24	70	18	64
16	8	72	25	45	16
42	56	15	10	54	42
40	35	7	90	20	40
27	100	16	28	50	27
30	14	9	60	49	30

See and Do

8x8	6x6	4x6			

Student's answer form

Student writes multiplication problem for products on grid.

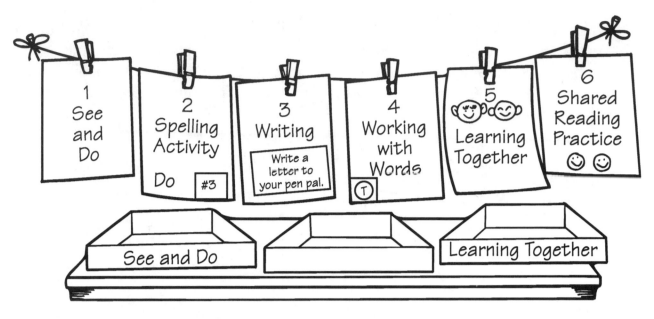

Combining Assigned and Enrichment Centers

Learning centers can provide activities that are within the scope of the regular curriculum such as practice and review. Centers can also focus on topics and materials that enrich and extend the curriculum.

1. **See and Do**
   See **page 183-185**.

2. **Spelling Activity**
   I posted a list of spelling activities in the classroom. Students look at the list and do activity that is assigned. To change, simply change the number of the activity that is assigned.

3. **Writing**
   Change the writing activity by attaching a new task to the center sign.

4. **Working with Words**
   This could be phonics, structural analysis, writing, and so on. This center is always called Working with Words but the activity changes each week.

5. **Learning Together**
   Each week this is a partner activity. Put the activity in the box by the center sign or clip a paper telling students what to do on the center sign.

6. **Shared Reading Practice**
   See **page 43**.

Note:
I used this set-up successfully in primary and intermediate classrooms. It does not take a lot of physical space. Activities are easy to change each week and some activities are permanent and available all or most of the year. You can use a generic checklist as shown. Plug your center ideas activities into this approach. The activities shown here are simply examples of one way I utilized this approach. Any time you want to do an activity together, simply clip on a Ⓣ to indicate Teacher as shown on center #4. See **page 187**.

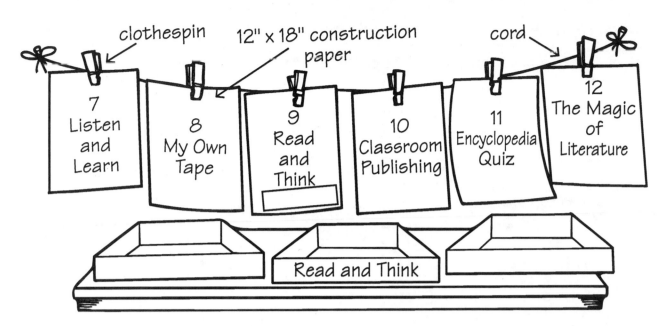

Generic Checklist

You can use this same checklist week after week. If you want to change one of your centers, change the sign and change the name on the checklist. On Mondays students staple the checklist inside their folders.

7. **Listen and Learn**
   Change task at listening center each week. See **page 176.**

8. **My Own Tape**
   Change task on My Own Tape sign at Listening center. See **page 176.**

9. **Read and Think**
   Plug in any reading activity you want students to do. If it is a paper and pencil activity, place worksheets on counter by the center sign.

10. **Classroom Publishing**
    See **page 188.**

11. **Encyclopedia Quiz**
    See **page 182.**

12. **The Magic of Literature**
    See **page 181.**

(Generic checklist)

★	Things To Do	M	Tu	W	Th	F✓
★	1. See and Do					
★	2. Spelling Activity					
★	3. Writing					
★	4. Working with Words					
★	5. Learning Together					
★	6. Shared Reading					
	7. Listen and Learn					
	8. My Own Tape					
	9. Read and Think					
	10. Classroom Publishing					
	11. Encyclopedia Quiz					
	12. Magic of Literature					

Name _____ Week of _____

Notes:

★ = required activity

Classroom Publishing - use all year

Students keep work in progress at the center, then work elsewhere.

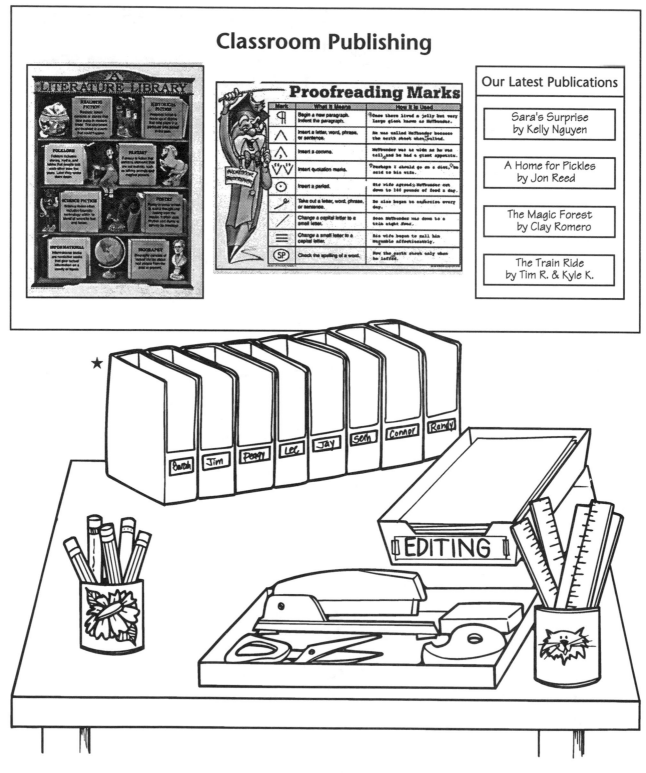

★ Box-it Storage System holds in-progress books.
   Cereal boxes, 1 per student, fastened together with brads.

NOTES

FS-8128 *100% Practical*

NOTES

Cooperative Learning

Cooperative learning can help build a sense of community in your classroom. It can create a caring feeling of helping, working, and learning together.

A Balanced Program for Your Students

Your learning day should be a balance of

- individual activities

- cooperative learning activities

- whole-class activities

Learning activities should be a balance of

- individual activities

- cooperative activities

- a few well-managed competitive activities

An effective learning program is balanced.

Teaching Students Cooperative Skills

For group activities to be cooperative-learning activities, students must

- participate individually

- exchange information

- recognize that everyone in the group is of equal importance

- develop cooperative skills

Teach your students how to work cooperatively.

Many students need to be taught how to take turns, consider others, and participate cooperatively as a member of a group. Invest time in establishing cooperative-learning procedures and behaviors so cooperative-learning activities in your classroom are of maximum value.

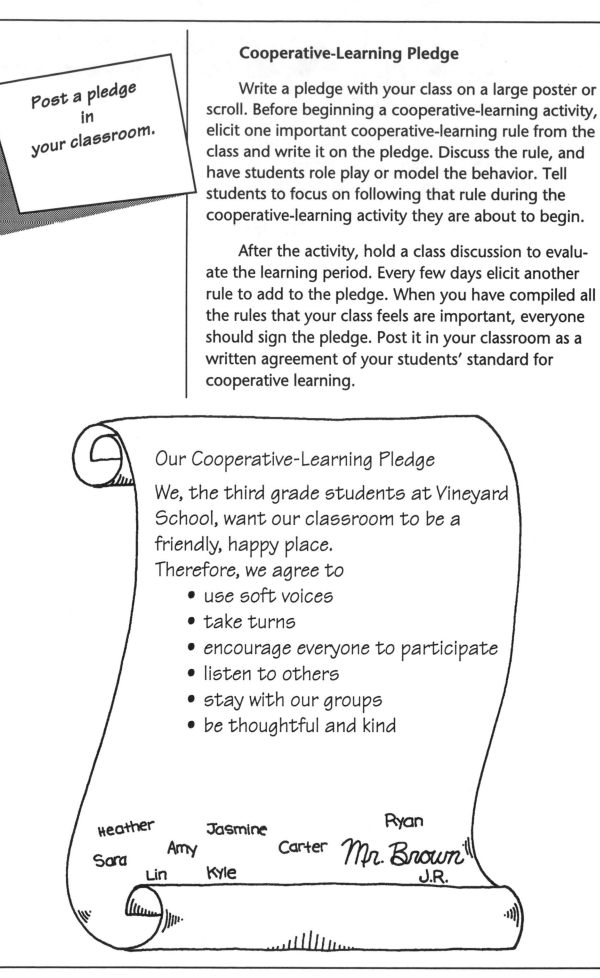

Post a pledge in your classroom.

Cooperative-Learning Pledge

Write a pledge with your class on a large poster or scroll. Before beginning a cooperative-learning activity, elicit one important cooperative-learning rule from the class and write it on the pledge. Discuss the rule, and have students role play or model the behavior. Tell students to focus on following that rule during the cooperative-learning activity they are about to begin.

After the activity, hold a class discussion to evaluate the learning period. Every few days elicit another rule to add to the pledge. When you have compiled all the rules that your class feels are important, everyone should sign the pledge. Post it in your classroom as a written agreement of your students' standard for cooperative learning.

Our Cooperative-Learning Pledge

We, the third grade students at Vineyard School, want our classroom to be a friendly, happy place.
Therefore, we agree to
- use soft voices
- take turns
- encourage everyone to participate
- listen to others
- stay with our groups
- be thoughtful and kind

Heather   Jasmine   Ryan
Sara   Amy   Carter Mr. Brown
   Lin   Kyle   J.R.

Grouping Students

Groups should be as heterogeneous as is possible for your mix of students. Consider gender, race, scholastic ability, and interests. Take a look at the management idea using magnets on **page 165** in **Chapter 9**.

Assigning Roles

Take time to explain and model roles so students understand what their individual responsibilities are. To ensure that everyone can instantly recognize group members' roles, use plastic pin-on name badges. Prepare sets of badges for cooperative-learning roles you use frequently. Some roles you may want to consider include:

- Reader: reads aloud to the group
- Writer/Recorder: writes down group ideas and answers
- Checker: makes sure everyone participates and completes assignment
- Materials Manager: gets materials/supplies for the group
- Summarizer: reviews what the group read or accomplished
- Encourager: encourages everyone to participate, praises group members
- Look at idea 3 on **page 102** in **Chapter 5** about assigning roles.

Make groups heterogeneous.

Rotate roles among students for different activities.

Learning Zones

Number paper plates from one to six. Use the plates to identify learning zones in your classroom. Post the signs in six different locations in your classroom. When they meet, group one meets in zone one, group two meets in zone two, and so on.

Cooperative-Learning Activities

Working in large cooperative-learning groups takes higher-level cooperative skills than working with a partner. Therefore, partner activities are an excellent way to help your students develop cooperative skills.

Partner Activities

Assign students to a learning partner for the month. Whenever you want to do a partner activity, students know who their partners are. At the beginning of each month, reassign learning partners. It's a good idea to list partners on the chalkboard.

1. Study Buddies

   Study buddies practice math facts, vocabulary, and spelling words together.

2. Reader and Writer

   Partners do a paper and pencil activity together. They take turns being reader and writer. Both students write their names on the paper. For example, if partners are doing a math worksheet, the reader reads the first problem aloud, the partners discuss the problem, the writer solves the problem and writes the answer. For the second problem, partners switch roles as reader and writer.

3. Summarize and Clarify

   Students work together reading and summarizing aloud. They take turns with roles of summarizer and clarifier. For example, if students are reading the science text, both students read the page or section. Then the summarizer explains what it was about. If the summarizer forgets something important, the other student mentions it. Then they both read the next page or section, and the other student takes a turn as summarizer. If your class subscribes to a classroom newspaper you can use it to summarize and clarify.

Begin with partner activities to build cooperative skills.

3. Checkmates

   In my classroom, checkmates were homework partners. Students were assigned a checkmate for the month. They checked their homework papers together, then stapled them together and placed them in the homework basket.

4. Literature Projects

   Many literature activities can work well as partner projects. Use projects such as making stick puppets, posters, bookmarks, and so on.

5. Q & A

   Partners can take turns asking each other questions. Each person gets to ask one question.

6. Information Exchange

   Partners tell each other the most important thing they learned following an activity.

Partner activities can make learning more fun.

Group Activities

1. Writing a Summary

   After reading or listening to a story or a chapter, a group of three students writes a three sentence summary. The summary will include a sentence about the beginning, middle, and ending of the story. Students discuss the story. Then each student is responsible for writing one of the three sentences of the summary. Each student writes his or her initials in parentheses after the sentence.

Cooperative learning helps students assume responsibility.

The bears go for a walk. (J.G.)
Goldilocks falls asleep in the house. (K.R.)
The bears come home and find her! (L.S.)

2. Team Work

Use this cooperative-learning activity with worksheets. Divide your class into groups that have exactly the same number of students. (It can be three, four, or five students—whatever divides evenly into your class size.) Groups sit together and each member has the same worksheet.

One student in each group reads the first question/problem aloud, the group discusses it and agrees on an answer. Students write on their individual papers. Then students compare papers and make sure everyone has the answer written correctly. Another student reads the next problem/question aloud. Each group works together reading, discussing, agreeing on an answer, writing, and comparing answers.

When each group completes the worksheet, one student in the group staples the group's papers together and gives them to the teacher. When papers have been stapled and turned in by all groups, the teacher announces which paper in the packets will be graded. For example, you might announce that you are going to mark the third paper in each packet. All papers in the packet receive the same grade as the third paper.

It is important to tell your class ahead of time that you plan to grade papers in this manner. Students make sure that everyone's paper is completed accurately.

Team work is a highly successful cooperative-learning activity.

3. Reciprocal Teaching

This discussion activity works well with literature books with chapters. Group students into sections that remain constant throughout the reading of the chapter book. After reading the first chapter, one student in the group is the leader. That student takes the group through three steps shown on the chart. A different student is the leader for the next chapter.

Reciprocal teaching works well with literature.

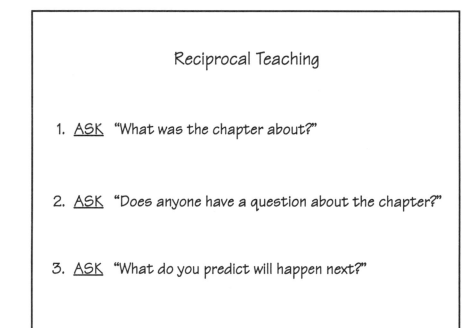

Reciprocal Teaching

1. ASK "What was the chapter about?"

2. ASK "Does anyone have a question about the chapter?"

3. ASK "What do you predict will happen next?"

Cooperative learning benefits individual students because it allows them to develop necessary social skills, a tolerance for the ideas and views of others, and can boost academic achievement. Cooperative learning will benefit your classroom because it fosters peer support and team spirit. There are cooperative-learning activities included in most chapters of this book.

NOTES

FS-8128 *100% Practical*

The ideas in this chapter are adaptable to your teaching style.

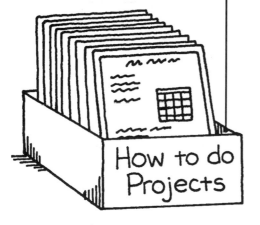

How to do Projects

Learning Activities and Projects

In this chapter, step-by-step directions are provided for a variety of activities and projects. Each page has easy-to-follow directions for a different activity. Directions are simplified so students can use them and work independently. Use these pages in whichever ways best suit your teaching style.

1. Refer to this chapter for ideas.

2. Photocopy the directions for students who are working on projects at home.

3. Make "How to Do Projects" cards by making a photocopy of each page. Mount each page on construction paper or oak tag. File the "How to Do Projects" cards in a box for students to use.

4. When you want to give your class a choice of activities, display several "How to Do Projects" cards and let students choose the activity they wish to do.

Choose 1 project

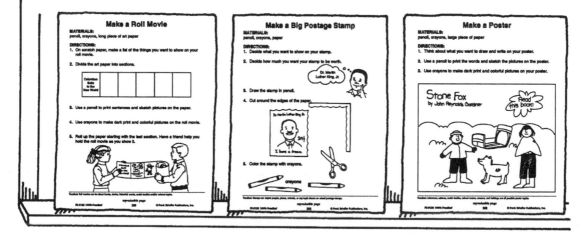

Students can keep track of the projects they complete throughout the year. Use the reproducible form on the following page.

My Project List

_____
Name

Projects I've Done	Date

Make Stick Puppets

MATERIALS:

pencil, crayons, construction paper, drawing paper, tape, pages from magazines

DIRECTIONS:

1. Place two magazine pages on your desk.

2. Fold over the bottom corner.

3. Roll.

4. Fasten the corner with tape to make a stick for the puppet.

tape

5. Make a puppet out of paper. Tape it to the paper stick.

Teacher: Students can make puppets of famous people or characters from literature.

reproducible page

© Frank Schaffer Publications, Inc.   201   FS-8128 *100% Practical*

Make a Poster

MATERIALS:

pencil, crayons, large piece of paper

DIRECTIONS:

1. Think about what you want to draw and write on your poster.

2. Use a pencil to print the words and sketch the pictures on the poster.

3. Use crayons to make dark print and colorful pictures on your poster.

Make a Book Jacket

MATERIALS:

pencil, crayons, construction paper

DIRECTIONS:

1. Fold the paper as shown.

2. On the front cover:
   - Write the title and author.
   - Draw a colorful picture.

3. On the back cover:
   - Write your opinion of the book and sign your name.
   - Ask other students who have read the book to write comments about the book.

4. On the flaps:
   - Write a sentence about the book.
   - Write about the author.

reproducible page

Make a Display in a Box

MATERIALS:
box, construction paper, drawing paper, crayons, paste

DIRECTIONS:
1. Cover the inside and outside of the box with construction paper.

2. Think about the scene you want to make inside the box. Use paper, foil, clay, twigs, pebbles and other objects to create the scene.

3. Write about your display in a box on papers and paste the papers on the outside of the box.

Teacher: Box displays might show a scene from a book, an animal in its habitat, or a scene from history.

reproducible page

Make a Roll Movie

MATERIALS:
pencil, crayons, long piece of art paper

DIRECTIONS:
1. On scratch paper, make a list of the things you want to show on your roll movie.

2. Divide the art paper into sections.

Columbus Sails to the New World				

3. Use a pencil to print sentences and sketch pictures on the paper.

4. Use crayons to make dark print and colorful pictures on the roll movie.

5. Roll up the paper starting with the last section. Have a friend help you hold the roll movie as you show it.

Teacher: Roll movies can be about books, stories, historical events, social studies and/or science topics.

reproducible page

Make a Picture Dictionary

MATERIALS:

pencil, crayons, construction paper, art paper

DIRECTIONS:

1. Make a list of the words you want to put in your dictionary.

2. Number words in alphabetical order on scratch paper.

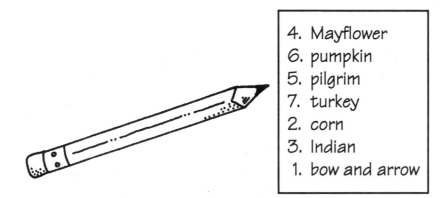

4. Mayflower
6. pumpkin
5. pilgrim
7. turkey
2. corn
3. Indian
1. bow and arrow

3. Make a booklet with construction-paper covers.

4. Write the words in the dictionary in alphabetical order and draw a colorful picture for each word.

pilgrim

pumpkin

5. Decorate the covers of your dictionary.

Make a Paper Quilt

MATERIALS:

pencil, crayons, art paper

DIRECTIONS:

1. Choose a topic for your paper quilt. Think about what you want to show on the quilt.

2. Divide the art paper in squares for the quilt.

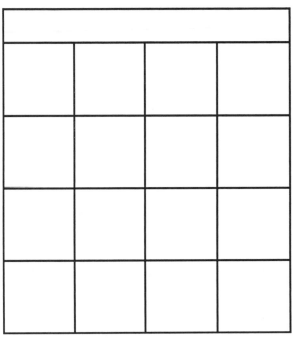

3. Draw colorful pictures in the squares on the quilt.

Teacher: Topics for paper quilts can include literature, months, holidays, seasons, all about me, science, and social studies.

reproducible page

Make a Big Postage Stamp

MATERIALS:

pencil, crayons, paper

DIRECTIONS:

1. Decide what you want to show on your stamp.

2. Decide how much you want your stamp to be worth.

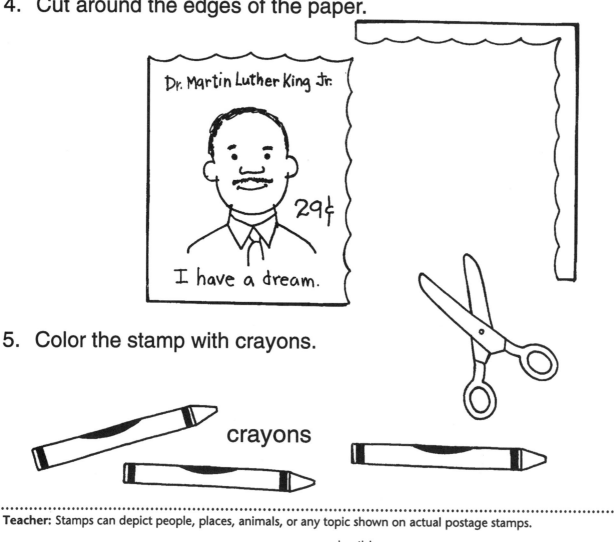

3. Draw the stamp in pencil.

4. Cut around the edges of the paper.

5. Color the stamp with crayons.

crayons

Teacher: Stamps can depict people, places, animals, or any topic shown on actual postage stamps.

reproducible page

Make a Large Picture Postcard

MATERIALS:

pencil, crayons, art paper or oak tag

DIRECTIONS:

1. Think about the picture you want to draw on the postcard. Decide if you want to have any words on the front of the postcard.

2. On the front of the card:
   • Use a pencil to sketch the picture.
   • Color the picture.

3. On the back of the postcard:
   • Write about the picture in the upper left-hand corner.
   • Write a note on the card.
   • Draw a stamp.
   • Write an address on the card.

Sonoma County is one hour north of San Francisco.

Dear Mrs. Kenwood,

Love,
Mimi

To
Mrs. Kenwood
6 Glen Ellen Dr.
Healdsburg, CA
55555

Teacher: Postcards can show a variety of places and topics.

reproducible page

Make a Small Cube

MATERIALS:

pencil, crayons, construction paper, art paper, small square box
(from tissues)

DIRECTIONS:

1. Paste construction paper on the cube.

2. There are six sides on the cube. Think about what you want to put on the cube.

3. Draw pictures or write on paper. Paste your pictures and writing on the cube.

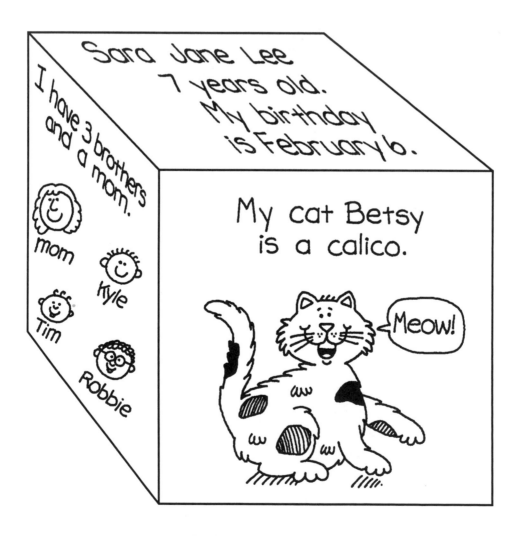

Teacher: Cubes can focus on poetry, all about me, books, social studies, or science.

reproducible page

Make a Large Cube

MATERIALS:
pencil, crayons, six 12" x 12" squares of oak tag, six 12" x 12" pieces of art paper, tape

DIRECTIONS:
1. Think about the topic you will show on the cube. Think about what you want to draw and write on the six sides of the cube.

2. Use pencil to draw and write on the art paper. Use crayons to color the pictures and words.

3. Paste the art-paper squares on the oak-tag squares. Tape into a cube.

Teacher: Large cubes can be made by individuals or cooperative-learning groups. Cube themes can be about literature, social studies, and science.

reproducible page

Make a Story Board

MATERIALS:
pencil, crayons, large piece of oak tag or bulletin-board paper

DIRECTIONS:
1. Make a list of the things you want to show on your story board.

2. Number the items on the list in the order you want to show them on the story board.

3. Divide the large piece of paper into the number of sections you need.

4. Write and draw colorful pictures on the story board.

Colonial America	1	2	3
4	5	6	7
8	9	10	11
12	13	14	by Brenna Blake Ryan

Teacher: Story boards can be about literature, social studies, and science.

reproducible page

Make a Parade Float

MATERIALS:

pencil, crayons, construction paper, art paper, shoe box, cereal or cracker box

DIRECTIONS:

1. Cover the box with construction paper.

2. Decorate the box like a float in a parade. You can use paper scraps, foil, clay, twigs, pebbles, and other objects on the float.

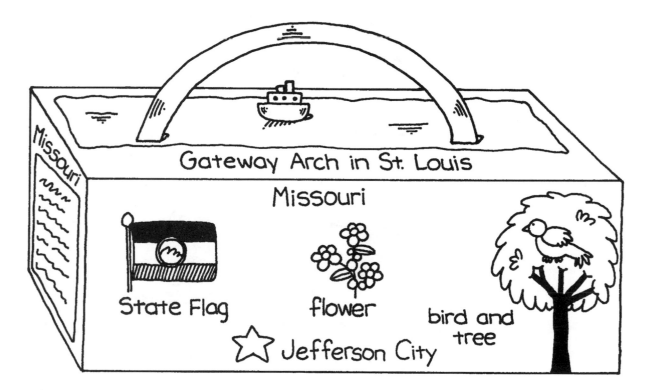

reproducible page

Make a Labeled Diagram

MATERIALS:

pencil, crayons, art paper

DIRECTIONS:

1. Use pencil to draw the object.

2. Label the object.

3. Label the parts of the object.

4. Color the picture you drew.

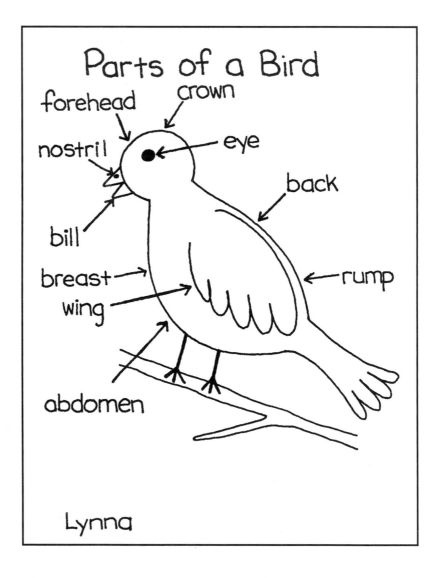

Teacher: Labeled diagrams can show insects, animals, flowers, and plants.

reproducible page

FS-8128 *100% Practical*   214   © Frank Schaffer Publications, Inc.

Make a Game Board

MATERIALS:

pencil, crayons, large piece of oak tag or bulletin-board paper, construction paper cut into 3" x 5" cards

DIRECTIONS:

1. Think about the topic for your game board and the kinds of questions you will write on the game cards.

2. Use scratch paper to sketch ideas for your game board. Then use pencil to draw the game board on a large piece of paper. Be sure to have a starting place and ending place for the game markers.

3. Write questions on the game cards.

4. Color the game board.

5. Write rules for playing the game on the back of the game board.

6. Make markers from construction paper in a variety of colors.

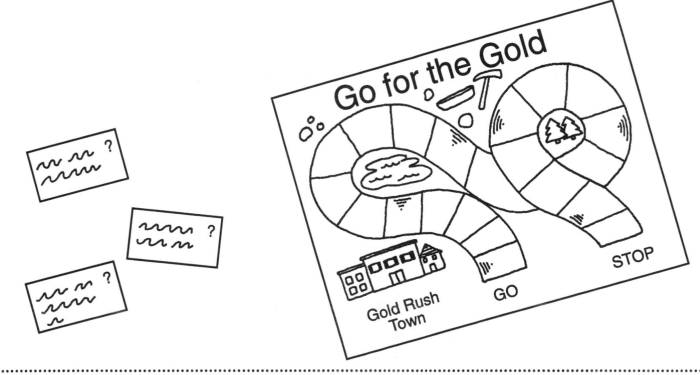

Teacher: Games can be about literature, social studies, or science topics. Cooperative-learning groups can create games.

reproducible page

Make an Accordion Book

MATERIALS:

pencil, crayons, long piece of butcher paper, cardboard, scissors.

DIRECTIONS:

1. Fold the paper in half the long way.

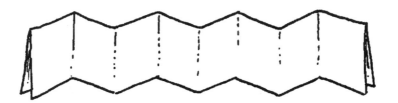

2. Accordion-fold the paper into an even number of sections.

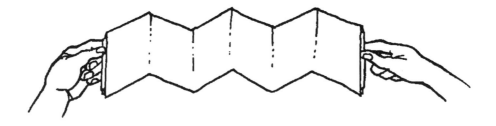

3. Insert a piece of cardboard into each end. Tape the corners.

4. Write and illustrate a story or poem.

Make a Flap Book

MATERIALS:
pencil, crayons, paper, scissors, glue

DIRECTIONS:
1. Write a story about something that is lost or hidden.

2. Plan illustrations that will show the lost thing under a flap.

3. To make a flap, cut out the shape of something in the illustration.

4. Fold back one edge of the flap shape. Glue it to the illustration. Show the lost thing under the flap.

reproducible page

FS-8128 *100% Practical*

Make a Shape Book

MATERIALS:

pencil, crayons, two sheets of construction paper, writing paper, scissors, hole punch, yarn or metal rings

DIRECTIONS:

1. Trace a shape on construction paper to make front and back covers. Cut them out.

2. Trace the shape onto writing paper to make pages.

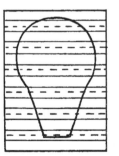

3. Write and illustrate your story.

4. Punch holes in the pages and covers. Put them together with yarn or metal rings.

reproducible page

Make a Pop-up Book

MATERIALS:

crayons, construction paper, scissors, glue

DIRECTIONS:

1. Write a story. Plan illustrations showing pop-up characters.

2. Fold a small strip of paper into fourths. Unfold. Then refold the strip so it makes a box shape.

3. Fold a sheet of paper in half. Glue the box shape to the paper at the fold. Draw the background on the paper.

4. Color and cut out a pop-up character. Glue it to the box shape. Write on the pages.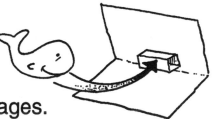

5. Make other pages. Glue them back to back. Glue the pages into a cover.

reproducible page

Make a Tall Book

MATERIALS:

pencil, crayons, construction paper, drawing paper, stapler

DIRECTIONS:

1. Fold the drawing paper the long way to make pages.

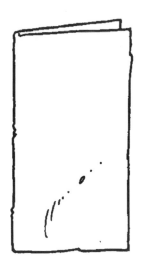

2. Make a cover by folding the construction paper the long way.

3. Place the pages inside the cover and staple them together near the fold.

4. Write and illustrate a story about something tall.

reproducible page

Make a Tiny Book

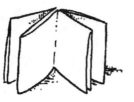

MATERIALS:
pencil, crayons, 8½" x 11" white paper

DIRECTIONS:
1. Fold the paper into eights. Unfold.

2. Refold halfway.

3. Cut on Middle fold halfway in. Unfold.

4. Fold in half lengthwise. Push ends toward middle.

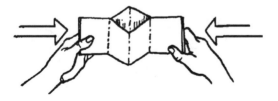

5. Push until the ends meet. Fold the left end towards the right.

6. Write a story in the book.

reproducible page

Make Easy Book Covers

Here are three ways to make covers.

MATERIALS:

scissors, stapler, tagboard, construction
paper, colored tape, hole punch, metal rings, yarn

STAPLED COVER

1. Staple the pages together.
2. Cut out cover pieces that are
   $\frac{1}{2}$ inch bigger than the pages.
3. Place the pages inside the
   covers and staple.
4. Cover the staples with
   colored tape.

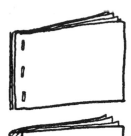

RING COVER

1. Cut out cover pieces that are
   $\frac{1}{2}$ inch bigger than the pages.
2. Punch two holes through the
   covers and pages.
3. Put the pages and covers
   together with rings.

TIED COVER

1. Cut out cover pieces that are
   $\frac{1}{2}$ inch bigger than the pages.
2. Punch three holes through the covers
   and pages.
3. Thread the ends of a piece of yarn
   down through the top and bottom
   holes.
4. Bring the ends up through the
   middle hole.
5. Tie a double-knotted bow on top.

reproducible page

Make Cloth Book Covers

MATERIALS:
paper for book pages, scissors,
cardboard, cloth, glue mixture (half water, half glue,)
darning needle and thread, 2-inch paintbrush

DIRECTIONS:

1. Fold the paper for the pages in half.

2. Cut two pieces of cardboard $\frac{1}{2}$ inch
   larger than the folded pages.

3. Cut out a piece of cloth $1\frac{1}{2}$ inches larger
   than the two pieces of cardboard.

4. Brush the glue mixture onto the
   cardboard and glue it to the cloth,
   leaving a small space in the middle.

5. Cut off the corners of the cloth.

6. Brush the glue mixture onto the edges
   of the cardboard. Fold the edges of the
   cloth over.

7. Press the cover flat and let it dry.

8. Sew the pages together down
   the center.

9. Brush the glue mixture onto the first
   and last pages and glue them to the
   inside covers.

reproducible page

         FS-8128 *100% Practical*

NOTES

Evaluation and Assessment

There are many strategies for assessing students' strengths and weaknesses. Assessment should have a connection to what is being taught and what students are learning.

Standardized Tests

Most districts use standardized tests and publish the results in community newspapers. Unfortunately, many people outside of education look at test scores as the sole indicator of pupil and school success. Like many educators, I regard standardized test scores as merely one of many indicators of progress.

Standardized tests are only one indicator of progress.

The Portfolio Approach

Portfolios are powerful assessment tools. They can take many forms. Well-managed, organized portfolios can provide a broad picture of student strengths and weaknesses.

Portfolios offer a different look at progress.

> Portfolios are great for sharing individual progress with parents.

Definition and Purpose of Portfolios

A portfolio contains a carefully gathered selection of an individual student's work. The purpose of portfolios is to show progress over time. For example, at the end of the year you can compare writing samples from the beginning, middle, and end of the year.

How Portfolios Are Used

Portfolios should be shared with parents at conferences. They are reviewed by students and teachers throughout the year. Portfolios should follow the students through the grades.

Some teachers send portfolios home every 8 or 10 weeks with a cover letter telling parents that students will explain the portfolio to them. After they peruse the portfolios together, the work is returned to school intact.

Organizing Portfolios

Create two portfolios for each student. Make a *Language Portfolio* and a *Grade-Level Portfolio* for each student. At the end of the school year, combine these portfolios into one that moves on with the student.

Having two portfolios throughout the school year makes portfolios easier to handle and manage because they contain less material. The *Language Portfolio* contains materials that pertain to reading, writing, and language. The *Grade-Level Portfolio* contains materials on subjects other than language. Place a stamp pad and date stamp by the portfolios. It comes in handy for dating materials that are added to portfolios by teachers and students.

> **Keep separate portfolios, then combine them at year's end.**

Contents of Portfolios

Look over this list of items you can include in students' portfolios. Be certain to date all entries.

1. Teacher Notes/Comments

   You can keep teacher notes on adhesive labels, in a spiral notebook, or a binder. Choose the method that will work best for you.

> **Portfolios can be designed to accommodate many needs.**

Adhesive Labels

Adhesive labels can be used for teacher notes. Labels are available in office-supply stores and many educational-supply stores.

Place a sheet of labels on your clipboard at the beginning of a week. Print each student's name on a label. Keep the clipboard handy so by the end of the week you will have jotted a comment on each student's label. Be sure to write the date on the label as well.

At the end of the week, remove each student's label and affix it to a piece of paper in the portfolio labeled Teacher Notes as shown. There are 36 weeks in a school year. If you record observations about students once a week, at the end of the year you will have 36 dated entries for each student.

Adhesive labels are handy for teacher notes.

Be sure to date all your notes.

Kira B.

Teacher Notes

Kira   9-27-94
Good job on rewrite.

Kira   10-4-94
Watch those
punctuation marks.

Spiral Notebook

Use a thick spiral notebook. Make a masking-tape tab for each student, allowing several pages of lined paper for each. If you have a writing conference with each student at least once a week, you can use this notebook to jot comments about students' writing.

At the end of the year, remove each student's pages, staple them together, and add them to the portfolio. To make sure you make a notation about each student, keep track on a class list. A reproducible class record form is provided on **page 99** in **Chapter 5**.

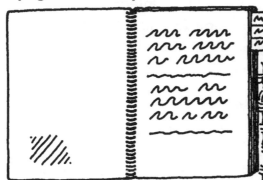

Three-ring Binder

Another method is to reproduce the Teacher Notes form on **page 234**, making several pages for each student. Place these pages in a three-ring binder and add tabs with students' names. You can use the three-ring binder in the same way as the spiral notebook described above.

> Teacher notebooks keep everything in one place.

Copies of interest inventories and book lists are an easy way to add dimension to portfolios.

Select representative samples of work for placement in a portfolio.

Staple students' first drafts to final copies and place in portfolios.

2. Interest Inventories

A reproducible general-interest inventory is provided on **page 235**, and a reading interest inventory on **page 236**. Place interest inventories in students' portfolios.

3. My Book List/Log

Students are responsible for keeping a list of literature they read throughout the year. A reproducible book list is provided on **page 237**. **Pages 238–239** offer reproducible forms on which students may respond to books. Reproduce copies of **page 240** to provide a motivating reading log. Monkeys may be hooked together to form a chain as students read, then unhooked and gathered for inclusion in a student's portfolio.

4. Teacher-Selected Samples of Students' Work

Do not try to place every piece of a child's work in his or her portfolio—obviously this would make it unwieldy. After reviewing several works, place selected samples in the portfolio. Mark *TS* (teacher selected) on the upper right-hand corner of each sample you select for portfolios. Emphasize quality over quantity. For example, from a sampling of a student's writings, select one that is most representative or revealing about the student to place in the portfolio. Jot a note on the sample telling why it was selected.

5. Student-Selected Samples of Work

Let students select samples to place in the portfolio. Have them mark *SS* (student selected) on the upper right-hand corner of each sample they select. Students should have a reading/ writing/language work folder where they save completed work from the week.

At the end of the week, students go through the collection of work in the folder and select a piece for their language portfolios. You can ask students to select a piece that falls into a specific category:

• their best work

• the piece that is most creative

• the assignment that was most difficult

Have students attach a note to the piece they select telling how and why it was selected.

When you place a limit on the number of pieces a student can add to his/her portfolio, students are more selective and analytical.

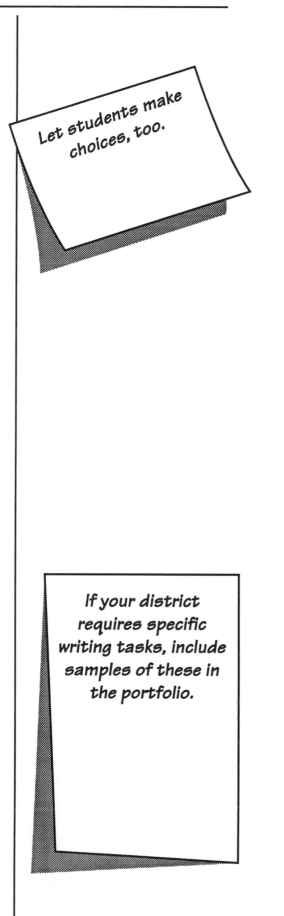

Let students make choices, too.

If your district requires specific writing tasks, include samples of these in the portfolio.

6. Timed-Writing Samples

Some school districts have established writing tasks for specific grade levels. For instance, in February, all fourth-grade students have 15 minutes to write a paragraph describing the school playground. This timed writing sample, done by all fourth-grade students in the district, is placed in all fourth-grade students' folders.

Appropriate timed-writing activities can be established for each grade level.

7. Tests and Test Scores

Include records of tests in students' portfolios.

> Audiotapes can provide a chronological record of students' oral-reading progress.

8. Audiotapes

   If each student is provided with a blank audio-cassette tape, students can record themselves reading aloud. Students should begin the taping activity by stating the date the sample is recorded.

   At the end of the year, tapes will reflect chronological samples of oral reading. Perhaps students could take tapes home for parents to hear and then return them to school. Take a look at the idea on **page 133** for more ideas about tape recording.

9. Journals

   Photocopy sample pages from students' journals and place them in portfolios.

10. Student Self-Evaluations

    Include self-evaluations in portfolios. In some classrooms, students complete self-evaluations at the end of each month or at the end of each quarter. Take a look at the reproducible self-evaluation forms on **pages 241** and **242**.

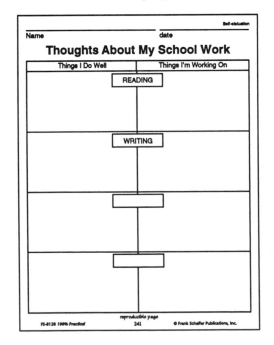

Managing Portfolios

Throughout the year, students and teachers need to remove extraneous materials from portfolios; otherwise, at the end of the year you have a time-consuming organizational task waiting to be done. Students should take part in managing and organizing their portfolios.

If you have two portfolios for each student (*Language* and *Grade-Level)* why not go through the box of *Language Portfolios* at the end of September? If you have several teacher-selected writing samples that are similar, choose one to keep in the portfolio and let the student take the extras home.

Let the student look through the samples he placed in the portfolio, and select a limited number to keep in the portfolio. In the end of October go through the *Grade-Level Portfolios* and remove some items.

If at the end of each month you go through one box of portfolios, each portfolio will have been reviewed every other month. At the end of the year they will be organized and the selection process will be completed. Then you can merge the two portfolios into one that goes with students to the next grade level.

Tests, grades, and portfolios should all be viewed as opportunities to get a more complete picture of your students' strengths and weaknesses.

Teacher Notes

Student _____

Date: _____ _____

_____

_____

_____

Date: _____ _____

_____

_____

_____

Date: _____ _____

_____

_____

_____

Date: _____ _____

_____

_____

_____

Date: _____ _____

_____

_____

_____

Date: _____ _____

_____

_____

_____

FS-8128 *100% Practical*   © Frank Schaffer Publications, Inc.

My name is _____

Today is _____

My Thoughts About School

1. My favorite school subject is _____

   because _____

   _____

2. The best thing about school is _____

   _____

   _____

3. The worst thing about school is _____

   _____

   _____

4. What is one thing you would change about _____ grade?

   _____

   _____

   _____

5. What do you like to do when you have free time out of school?

   _____

   _____

   _____

FS-8128 *100% Practical*

If You Ask Me...

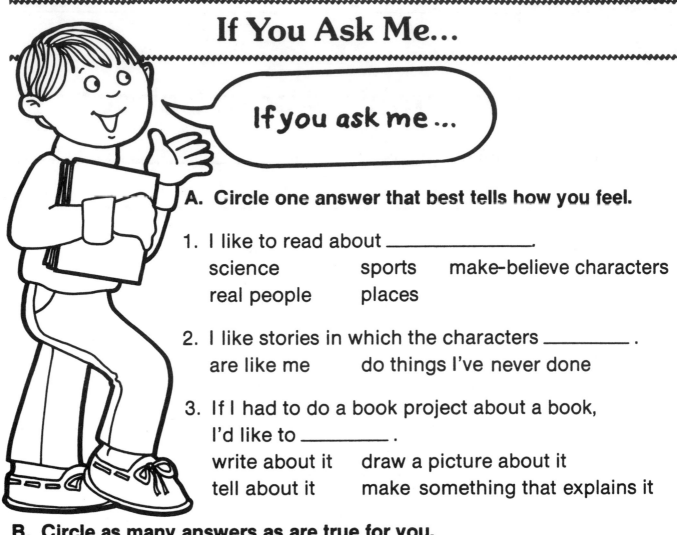

If you ask me ...

A. Circle one answer that best tells how you feel.

1. I like to read about _____.

    science   sports   make-believe characters
    real people   places

2. I like stories in which the characters _____.
    are like me   do things I've never done

3. If I had to do a book project about a book,
    I'd like to _____.
    write about it   draw a picture about it
    tell about it   make something that explains it

B. Circle as many answers as are true for you.

4. I've never read a book about _____.
    a famous person   history   people in other lands
    how to make something   science   how something works

5. I like to read _____.
    magazines   short stories   books   newspapers   poetry   plays

**C. Look at the following list. Underline the types of books you like to
read. Circle any types you are not familiar with.**

    hero stories   tall tales   ghost stories
    mysteries   myth   hobbies
    fables/fairy tales biographies   science fiction

Try This! What is the best book you have ever read? Write why.

reproducible page

Books I've Read

Titles and Authors

FS-8128 *100% Practical*

Book Review

Think carefully about a book you've read. How did it make you feel? Did you enjoy it? Why or why not? Answer the questions below to evaluate your feelings about the book.

Title of book _____

Author _____

1. How do you think the author wanted you to feel at the end of the story? _____

2. How did you feel? _____

3. Did the story hold your interest? _____
   Why or why not? _____

4. What did you like best about the story?

   _____

   _____

5. What did you like least? _____

   _____

   _____

6. Would you recommend this book to others? _____
   Why or why not? _____

   _____

7. Would you read another book by the same author? _____
   Why or why not? _____

   _____

Try This! Make a list of ten words that describe feelings you had while reading this book.

reproducible page

238

The Book Reporter

Vol. XXI, No.1   19____

_____   _____
Title   Author

Book Is Read Cover To Cover!

by _____

Description of the Character

_____

_____

_____

_____

Action scene from book

Events As They Happened

_____

_____

_____

_____

_____

_____

_____

_____

_____

A picture of the character

This Reporter's Opinion

_____

_____

_____

_____

_____

Try This! You are the "Star" Book Reporter and have been sent out to the scene of the book. Write where and when it took place.

Bananas About Books

Use this monkey as a reading log for a book. When you finish the book, color and cut out the monkey.

Use this monkey as a reading log for a book. When you finish the book, color and cut out the monkey.

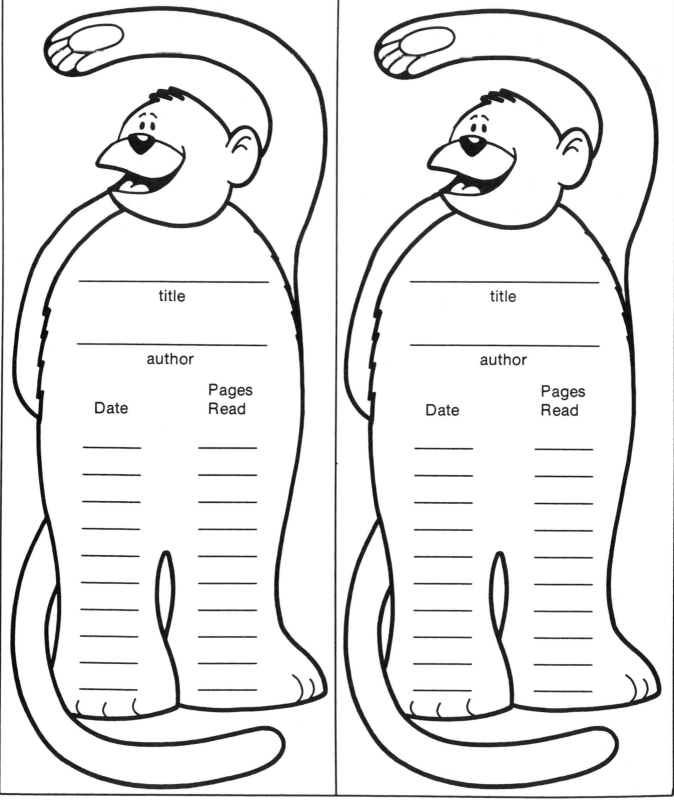

title

author

Date

Pages
Read

title

author

Date

Pages
Read

reproducible page

Name _____   date _____

Thoughts About My School Work

Things I Do Well	Things I'm Working On
READING	
WRITING	

FS-8128 *100% Practical*

My name is _____

Today is _____

My Feelings About School

How do you feel you are doing

as a reader?_____

_____

_____

as a writer? _____

_____

_____

at working by yourself? _____

_____

_____

at working with others? _____

_____

_____

as a student in _____ grade? _____

_____

_____

_____

NOTES

FS-8128 *100% Practical*

NOTES

Instant Messages From the Teacher

1. Rubber stamps come in handy! Get custom stamps made at quick-print or office-supply stores.

Mr. Dan Smith, Teacher

Please read, sign, and return this to school.

Rubber stamps and pre-printed messages on labels can save lots of time.

2. Have gummed return-address labels printed with messages you frequently write.

Dan Smith, Teacher
Apple School
5 Apple Drive
Redding, CA 55555

Please sign and return this to school.
D. Smith, Teacher

IMPORTANT
Please go over this
with your child.

Lesson Plans

Save time writing lesson plans with this slick trick. Cut a file folder in half to use as an overlay in your plan book. Cut windows so you can write in the plan book. Write the schedule and information that stays the same from week to week on the overlay as shown on the following page.

Cut lesson-plan writing with a simple plan-book overlay.

File Folder Overlay for Plan Book

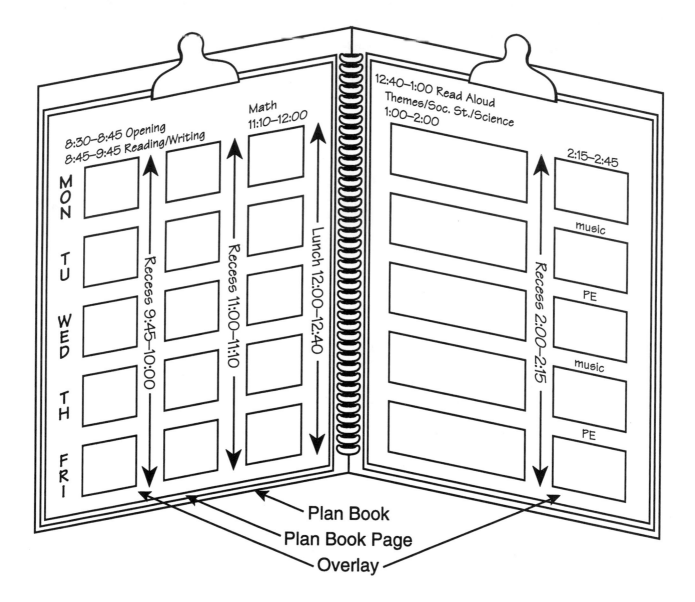

8:30–8:45 Opening
8:45–9:45 Reading/Writing

Math 11:10–12:00

MON
TU
WED
TH
FRI

Recess 9:45–10:00

Recess 11:00–11:10

Lunch 12:00–12:40

12:40–1:00 Read Aloud
Themes/Soc. St./Science
1:00–2:00

2:15–2:45

music

PE

music

PE

Recess 2:00–2:15

Plan Book

Plan Book Page

Overlay

Preparing for Substitutes

1. Instead of writing out lengthy plans, leave a tape-recorded message for your substitute. You still need to leave some written plans, but can record a myriad of details instead of writing them out.

Leave a tape-recorded message for your substitute.

2. Start a file folder for substitutes. When you have an activity left over at the end of the day or week that you did not have time to do, perhaps you can stash it in the folder for a substitute to use. Keep an eye out for activities to set aside. When you need to prepare for a substitute, select activities from this folder.

3. Make a seating chart in a file folder. Write students' names on stick-on notes. This comes in handy for your substitute all day long. You can use it when you want to reassign students' seats. Move the stick-on notes around until you come up with a seating plan that suits you. Then have students move to their "new" seats.

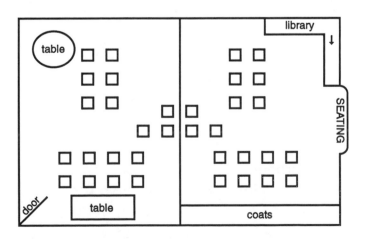

Using stick-on notes on seating charts makes changes easy.

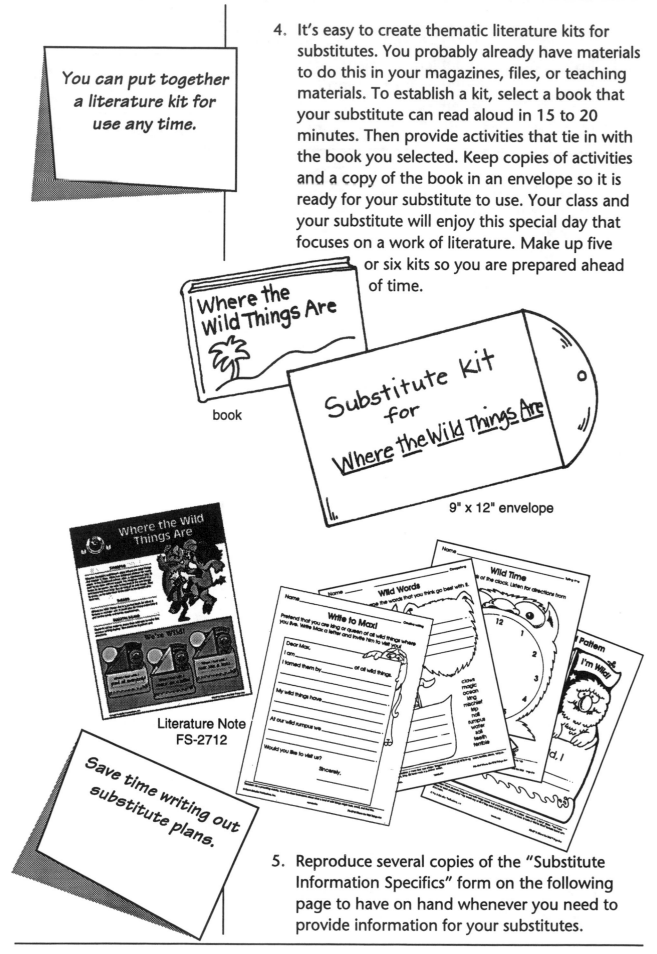

You can put together a literature kit for use any time.

4. It's easy to create thematic literature kits for substitutes. You probably already have materials to do this in your magazines, files, or teaching materials. To establish a kit, select a book that your substitute can read aloud in 15 to 20 minutes. Then provide activities that tie in with the book you selected. Keep copies of activities and a copy of the book in an envelope so it is ready for your substitute to use. Your class and your substitute will enjoy this special day that focuses on a work of literature. Make up five or six kits so you are prepared ahead of time.

Where the Wild Things Are

book

Substitute Kit for Where the Wild Things Are

9" x 12" envelope

Literature Note FS-2712

Save time writing out substitute plans.

5. Reproduce several copies of the "Substitute Information Specifics" form on the following page to have on hand whenever you need to provide information for your substitutes.

Substitute Specifics

Today you are substituting for _____ , grade _____ .

You can find these items located in the following spots:

Lesson plans/schedule _____ Grade book _____

Teacher's manuals _____ Seating chart _____

Emergency procedures chart _____

Student emergency information _____

A colleague who can help you is _____ in room _____ .

Special duties I have during the week include:

Monday _____

Tuesday _____

Wednesday _____

Thursday _____

Friday _____

These are usual routines for:

Lunch count _____

Restroom use_____

Dismissal_____

These students leave the classroom during the week for special classes or appointments.

	Students	Class/Reason	Time
Mondays			
Tuesdays			
Wednesdays			
Thursdays			
Fridays			

Other information _____

reproducible page

Organizing Magazines for Teachers

Organize your magazines by filing them in boxes according to season. Boxes will eventually contain a variety of magazines from several years. When you need ideas for back-to-school, all your fall magazines are in one box.

There are additional ideas for organizing magazines in Chapter 8, Using Themes, on **pages 146–147.**

> *A magazine file can be an invaluable resource.*

Organizing and Storing Charts

1. Hang charts on a space-saving hanger. Charts are easy to locate and remove from this chart holder.

2. Ask for a shipping box for charts at a school-supply store. Stores receive charts from manufacturers in cardboard boxes. Clip clothespins with titles on the charts. The box is free and keeps your charts in good condition.

3. Roll and clip charts with a clothespin. Write the title of charts on the clothespins. Store rolled charts in a box or basket.

> *Space-saver hangers are great for storing charts!*

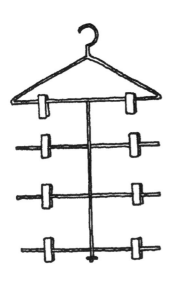

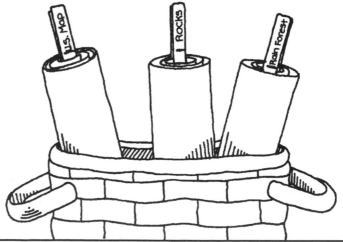

Organizing Your Classroom

1. Trace your left and right hand prints on signs to post in the right and left corners of the front wall of your classroom. Primary students can use this as a reference for right and left.

Hand print signs are easy to make.

2. Organize your classroom library with shoe boxes. Sort books into boxes to make them easier for students to find.

Shoe boxes make great book holders.

3. Make a set of plastic pin-on name tags for your class. Have students wear the name tags for:

   • field trips
   • substitutes
   • special assemblies
   • open house

   Reuse name tags from year to year by inserting different names.

Organizing Materials for Students

1. Establish a supply table where students can get paper, pencils, scissors, and other materials.

2. Use a cardboard tray (cut from a box) to hold stapler, staple remover, hole punch, and other materials you want to make available for students. Trace and label objects so students will put them back where they belong.

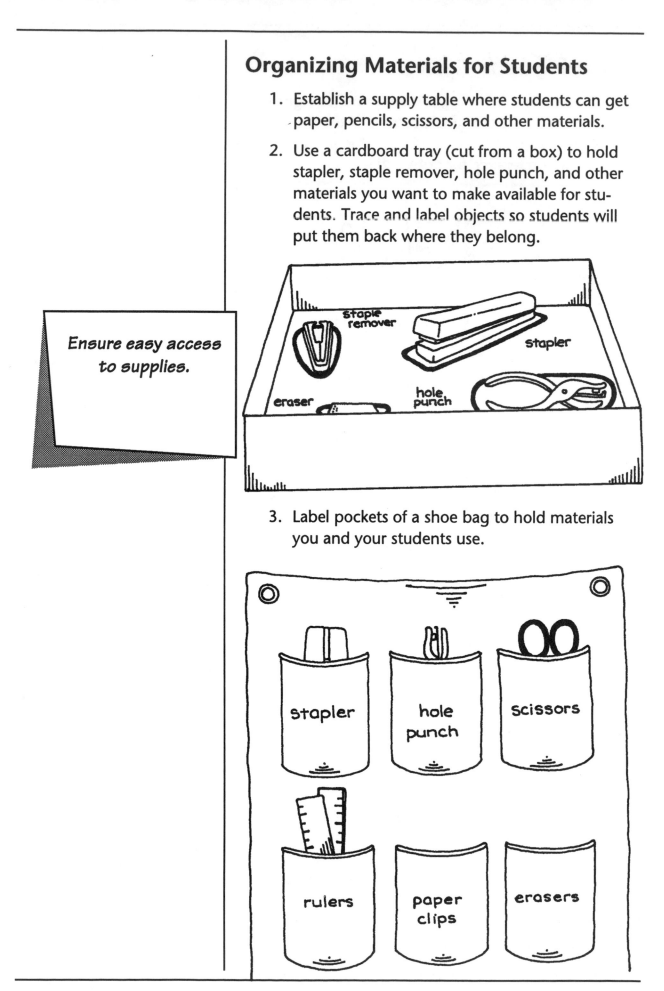

Ensure easy access to supplies.

3. Label pockets of a shoe bag to hold materials you and your students use.

Helping Students Work Efficiently

1. Use a timer occasionally in your classroom.

2. Help students better manage their time during paper and pencil activities. Divide the task into time segments and write checkpoints on papers as shown. This is especially helpful for students who are capable but have difficulty managing work time.

> Name _____
>
> 11:05
>
> 11:10
>
> ⓣ ____
>
> 11:15
>
> 11:20

3. To monitor a student's progress, put a "Teacher Checkpoint" on his paper. When the student arrives at the checkpoint, she must show the paper to the teacher. Teachers write their initials at the checkpoints.

    ⓣ *BL*

4. Before a recess or lunch break, have your students bring out the materials they will need after the break. When they return, you can begin without waiting for students to get ready.

Heighten Student Participation

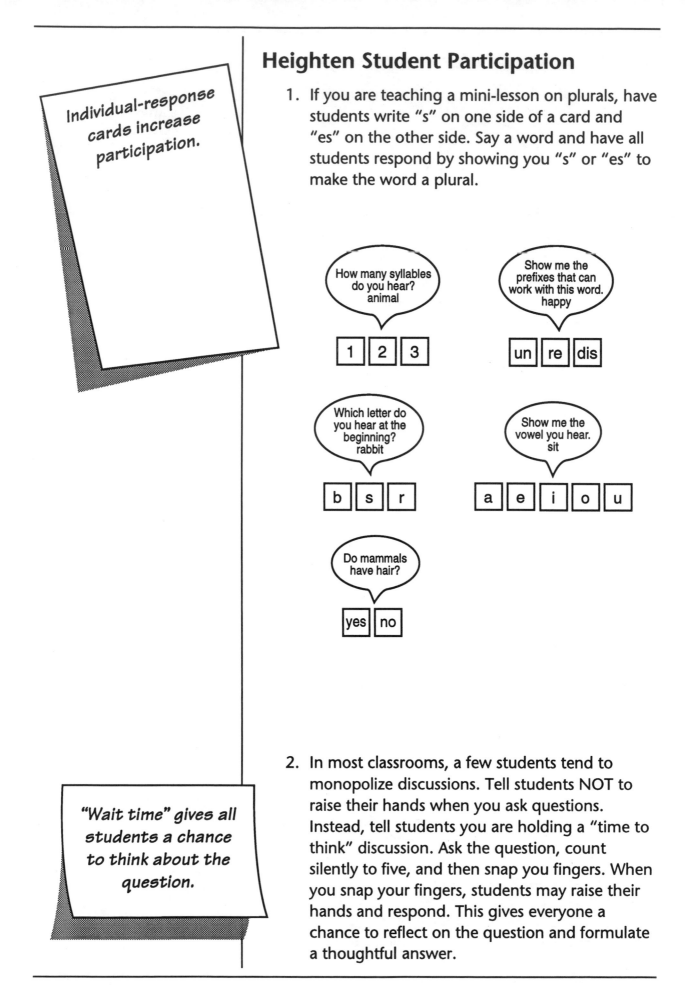

1. If you are teaching a mini-lesson on plurals, have students write "s" on one side of a card and "es" on the other side. Say a word and have all students respond by showing you "s" or "es" to make the word a plural.

How many syllables do you hear? animal

| 1 | 2 | 3 |

Show me the prefixes that can work with this word. happy

| un | re | dis |

Which letter do you hear at the beginning? rabbit

| b | s | r |

Show me the vowel you hear. sit

| a | e | i | o | u |

Do mammals have hair?

| yes | no |

2. In most classrooms, a few students tend to monopolize discussions. Tell students NOT to raise their hands when you ask questions. Instead, tell students you are holding a "time to think" discussion. Ask the question, count silently to five, and then snap you fingers. When you snap your fingers, students may raise their hands and respond. This gives everyone a chance to reflect on the question and formulate a thoughtful answer.

Individual-response cards increase participation.

"Wait time" gives all students a chance to think about the question.

3. Use "turn and teach" to gain 100 percent participation. Ask the class a question, then students turn to someone sitting near them and share answers to the question. Everyone gets to participate!

The most important thing I learned is that plants can be used to make medicines.

I learned that we have rain forests in the United States.

Give everyone a chance to respond.

4. Make sure you do not preface questions with a student's name. If you say a student's name, you are giving the group a cue as to who the question is for. Instead, ask the question and then state the name of the student whom you want to respond.

Why do you think Charlie said that? Michael?

Ways to Foster Independence

When students say "I don't get it," respond in a way that lets the student retain responsibility for problem solving. Here are some sample replies that encourage students to think about the problem in a different way.

"What else have you tried?"

"How can you help yourself?"

"Does that sound right to you?"

"Tell me what you are thinking."

Encourage students to think for themselves.

Ask a student who cheats how you can help him do his work independently.

How to Handle Cheating

Step 1. Take the student's paper. Jot a note on it stating what you observed and the date. Keep the paper.

Step 2. Confer privately with the student, asking why cheating was necessary. And ask students if they can think of ways cheating could be harmful to them—now or in the future.

Step 3. If cheating is an ongoing problem, confer with parents. Show parents the papers you have saved.

Getting Students to Put Their Names on Papers

1. Before collecting papers, have students touch their names on their papers.

2. Before collecting papers, have students follow one of these directions:

   • Highlight their names with yellow crayon.

   • Underline their names.

   • Make a box around their names.

   • Make a dotted line under their names.

   • Underline the vowels in their names.

These simple ideas will all but eliminate "no-name" papers.

3. Establish a "no-names" folder where you can place papers without names. When students are missing a paper they can check this folder for their work.

Collecting Students' Work

1. Establish work baskets for different subjects so papers/folders are sorted. Write "name" on one end of each basket as shown so students place their work in the basket right side up with their names at the top.

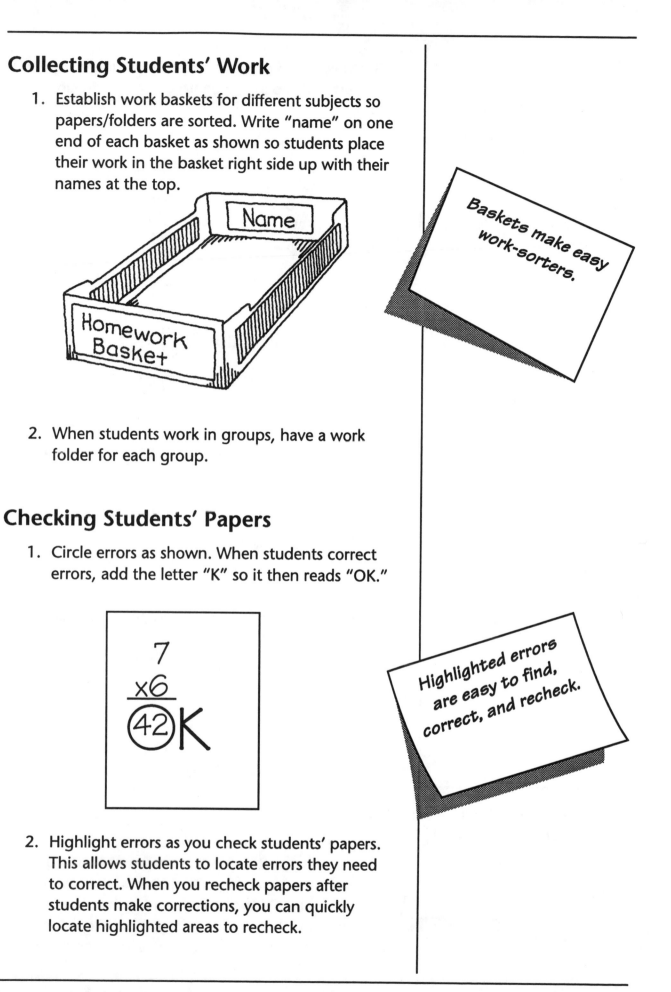

2. When students work in groups, have a work folder for each group.

Checking Students' Papers

1. Circle errors as shown. When students correct errors, add the letter "K" so it then reads "OK."

2. Highlight errors as you check students' papers. This allows students to locate errors they need to correct. When you recheck papers after students make corrections, you can quickly locate highlighted areas to recheck.

3. As you read through and check student papers, sort and clip into organized stacks with clothespins.

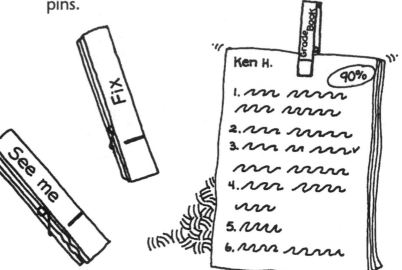

Providing Storage for Students' Work

1. Recycle cardboard boxes or purchase baskets, boxes, or hanging files.

2. Recycle cereal boxes into a storage system.

   This storage system is perfect for ongoing projects. It is pictured on **page 188** in **Chapter 9,** "Using Learning Centers."

3. Folders help students get organized and stay organized. Make work folders for students. See the folder ideas on **page 157** in **Chapter 8,** "Using Themes."

Helping Students Listen and Follow Directions

1. When you are ready to give directions, have your students assume a "listening posture." The listening posture is what you want your students to do as they listen. You might have your students fold their hands and look at you. Tell the class that when you say, "Time to listen," you want them to assume the listening posture.

2. When giving step-by-step directions, list the steps on the chalkboard. Number the steps. Read the directions aloud, pointing at each direction as you read it.

3. Have students repeat directions aloud as a group (like choral speaking).

4. Have students take turns explaining to partners what they are supposed to do.

5. As you go over written directions with students on a worksheet, have them underline or highlight (with a yellow crayon) key words.

6. Make a sign showing words frequently found in written directions. Glue actual objects on the sign as shown.

Help students develop skills for following directions.

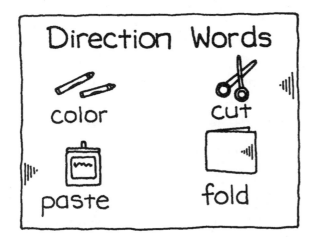

7. Write frequently stated directions on sentence strips. Clap your hands two times to signal the class you are holding up a strip with directions for students to read and follow. Read each direction aloud the first few times. Eventually you will be able to hold up strips and convey directions to your class without saying a word.

Signals are effective attention-getters.

8. Many students are in the habit of not listening as the teacher gives directions and then requesting individual help. Try this strategy to get students to tune in when you give directions. Tell students you will be giving them three minutes of independent work time. Give directions to your class and then set the timer for three minutes of independent work time. During the three-minute period tell students you are not available to answer questions and/or give individual help. When students know you will not be available, they listen more attentively.

Managing Students Who Need Your Help

1. On paper and pencil assignments, tell students to skip problems/questions they cannot answer and to complete everything possible on the paper. Then they can get help all at once on the parts of the paper they had difficulty with.

2. Write "I need help" on the chalkboard. Students sign up on the help list, skip the part they cannot do, and continue working. The teacher goes down the help list in sequence. Whenever possible, have students write the problem they are having difficulty with next to their names. Then you can help several students at once who are having difficulty with the same problem.

3. Establish a question chair in your classroom. When you are working with a group of students and someone has a question, he can sit quietly in the question chair. Move the question chair close to the group you are working with.

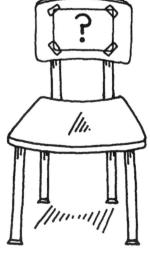

4. Make an open/closed sign. When you are working with a group and cannot be interrupted by other students, turn the sign to "closed." Flip it to "open" when you are available.

Photocopy Students' School Pictures

Make photocopies of students' photographs to use throughout the year. Color photographs will reproduce clearly in black and white. Use photocopies for

- pen-pal letters
- graphs
- scrapbooks
- yearbooks
- all-about-me activities
- publishing books (about the author)
- personal bookmarks

Use students' photos to personalize projects.

Classroom management is an integral part of your teaching day. The strategies given plus the reproducible pages that follow may help your classroom routine go smoothly.

Materials Manager

Item	Date Borrowed	By Whom	Date Returned

reproducible page

A Couple of Contracts

Challenge Contract

Date _____

I, _____ , accept the challenge to _____
(your name)

_____

_____ by _____

Signed _____
(your signature)

_____
(teacher's signature)

_____
(parent's signature)

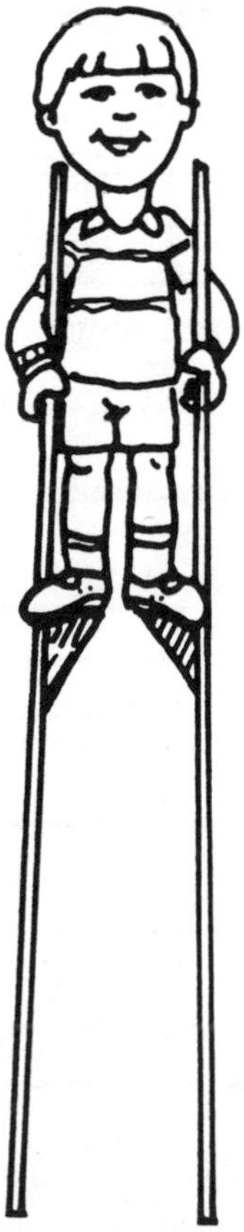

Boosting Behavior

Date _____

I, _____ , plan to

"boost" my behavior by _____

_____

_____

_____

_____

Signed _____
(your name)

Teacher's signature _____

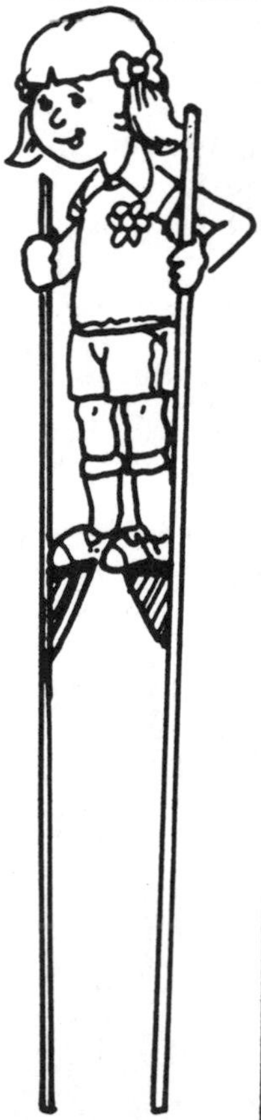

reproducible page

Make-up Work Memos

To _____ From _____ Date _____

Here are the "scoops" about the assignments you missed on _____

Math

Reading

Spelling/
Language

Science/
Social
Studies

Other

These assignments are due _____

A note to remind you...

THANKS!

reproducible page

Animal Awards

A Whale of an Accomplishment!

signature

You should be as proud as a peacock!

signature

You've done something to crow about!

signature

Give yourself a hand!

signature

FS-8128 *100% Practical*

Month of

Sunday	Monday	Tuesday	Wednesday	Thursday	Friday	Saturday

reproducible page

NOTES

FS-8128 *100% Practical*

NOTES

Communicating With School Families

Keeping school families informed is the responsibility of every teacher. Make it easy on yourself by setting up a "School-to-Home Communication" box or basket at the beginning of the school year.

Place a folder in the box for each month of the school year. Include a few extra folders in the back of the box.

When you are getting organized just before school starts, reproduce the parent communication forms you know you will use throughout the school year. Place the ready-to-use letters in your communication file. Sign the letters before you reproduce them so they are pre-signed. If possible, duplicate communication forms on colored paper.

Choose one color and use it throughout the year for all your school-to-home communication notices. Tell parents which color paper to watch for. This makes your messages easy for families to spot!

Organize information about students' families on the reproducible form on the following page.

Communicating with families encourages home-school support.

Home Information Sheet

Student's Name	Address	Home Phone #	Parents' Names	Other Phone #

reproducible page

Off to a Great Start!

Post a notice on the window of your classroom a week or so before school starts. Let visitors know how busy you are getting the classroom ready. Designate a certain time period for visitors to preview the room. Include pertinent information on your sign.

Encourage visitors, but set your own limits.

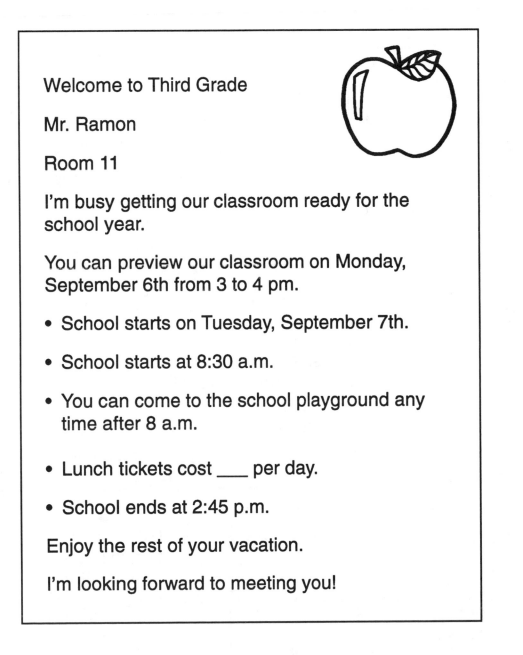

Welcome to Third Grade

Mr. Ramon

Room 11

I'm busy getting our classroom ready for the school year.

You can preview our classroom on Monday, September 6th from 3 to 4 pm.

- School starts on Tuesday, September 7th.

- School starts at 8:30 a.m.

- You can come to the school playground any time after 8 a.m.

- Lunch tickets cost ___ per day.

- School ends at 2:45 p.m.

Enjoy the rest of your vacation.

I'm looking forward to meeting you!

Take-Me-Home School Boxes

Collect lunch pails from the lost and found at your school at the end of the year. Once you have cleaned them out, you'll have colorful, sturdy boxes with handles. Fill the boxes and let students check them out. Halfway through the year, change the contents of the boxes. Show the boxes to families at back-to-school night so parents know they are available.

Lunch pails make handy containers for crayons, scissors, math manipulatives, and task cards. Below are several ideas for filling take-home boxes.

Reading
books
discussion questions
crayons
paper

Reading
book with story tape

To make tape, simply read the book aloud to your class. Tape record yourself as you read.

Math
task cards   paper
calculator   pencils
mail order   eraser
   catalog

Science
task cards
materials for a
   simple experiment
paper
pencils
magnifying glass

Writing
paper
shape book
   for writing
pencil
erasers
pens
stickers

Resources for Families

Start saving articles from newspapers, magazines, and educational journals that might be of interest to your students' families. Place articles in a binder, file folder, or magnetic photo album. Inform families you have a resource file available. Have the material on display at open house. Parents can peruse the file while they are waiting for conference appointments. Jot your name on articles and allow parents to borrow them to read carefully.

Keep families informed and involved.

Of Special Interest to Families

ABC's of School Behavior/My School Day

Reproduce the form at the top of **page 274**. Send this form home at the end of each week, every other week, or monthly as a report on students' behavior. See also the challenge contract and behavior booster forms in **Chapter 13, page 263**.

Reproduce the form at the bottom of **page 274**. Have students complete the form and take it home.

Feedback From Families

Give families an opportunity to provide feedback on how they feel the year is going for their children. Use the reproducible letter on **page 275**. Parents feel better about teachers and schools when they know their ideas and opinions are valued.

Name _____ Date _____

ABC's of School Behavior

| Attitude |

excellent   good   fair   poor

| Behavior |

excellent   good   fair   poor

| Cooperation |

excellent   good   fair   poor

Comments _____

_____   _____
Teacher's Signature   Parent's Signature
(Please sign and return.)

Name _____ Date _____

My School Day

I read _____

I practiced _____

I learned _____

_____

_____   _____
Teacher's Signature   Parent's Signature
(Please sign and return.)

reproducible page

Date _____

Dear Families,

At this time of year, I ask parents to share comments about how the school year is going. Your comments and concerns are important to me. From parent feedback, I can evaluate our program and consider changes and improvements. Your comments can help me better serve the needs of students and their families.

Please comment on the following areas:

1. Language Program (Reading and Writing) _____

_____

2. Math_____

_____

3. Social Studies/Science_____

_____

4. Classroom Management/Discipline_____

_____

Please complete the sentences below:

I like it when teachers_____

_____

You may want to consider changing_____

_____

I feel my child has made the least progress this year in_____

_____

I feel my child has made the most progress this year in_____

_____

You don't need to sign this form. You can mail it to school, drop it off in the office, or send it with your child to put in the classroom mail basket. Thanks for your help!

_____
Teacher

reproducible page

Family Newsletters

Families will be delighted to receive an informational newsletter that helps their children learn.

Ten ready-to-reproduce newsletters are provided—one for each month of the school year. Sign, reproduce, and send these informative newsletters home throughout the year.

You can send the letters at any time. If you wish to use them as monthly newsletters, you may want to use them in the sequence below.

Month	Topic
September	*Back-to-School Activities,* **page 277**
October	*Reading Activities,* **page 278**
November	*Math Activities,* **page 279**
December	*Gifts Students Can Make,* **page 280**
January	*Learning Activities,* **page 281–282**
February	*Talking About School,* **page 283**
March	*Parent Conferences,* **page 284**
April	*Homework Hints,* **page 285**
May	*Writing Activities,* **page 286**
June	*Learning Activities,* **page 287–288**

Reproduce the letters ahead of time and store them in your communication file. Or, place one copy of each letter in your file, where they'll be easy to find and use.

> *Send communication home at least monthly. These ready-to-go letters make it easy.*

School to Home
NEWSLETTER

_____
Date

Dear Families,

Our school year is off to a great start! Your child will be learning many new important skills this year. The suggestions below will help your child.

- Help your child develop a love for reading by reading aloud. Reading aloud is valuable even when students can read on their own.

- Help your child get a library card. Encourage your child to set aside a time for reading each day.

- Establish a "home office" for your child where he/she can do homework. Perhaps you can supply some office supplies like paper, pencils, pencil sharpener, erasers, and so on.

- Establish a container or place where your child puts all the items that must be taken to school. This helps children be better organized.

- Ask your child to tell you about the schoolwork he/she brings home. Take time to look through schoolwork with your child.

We are partners in your child's learning. Helping your child learn is important and fun for everyone!

_____
Teacher

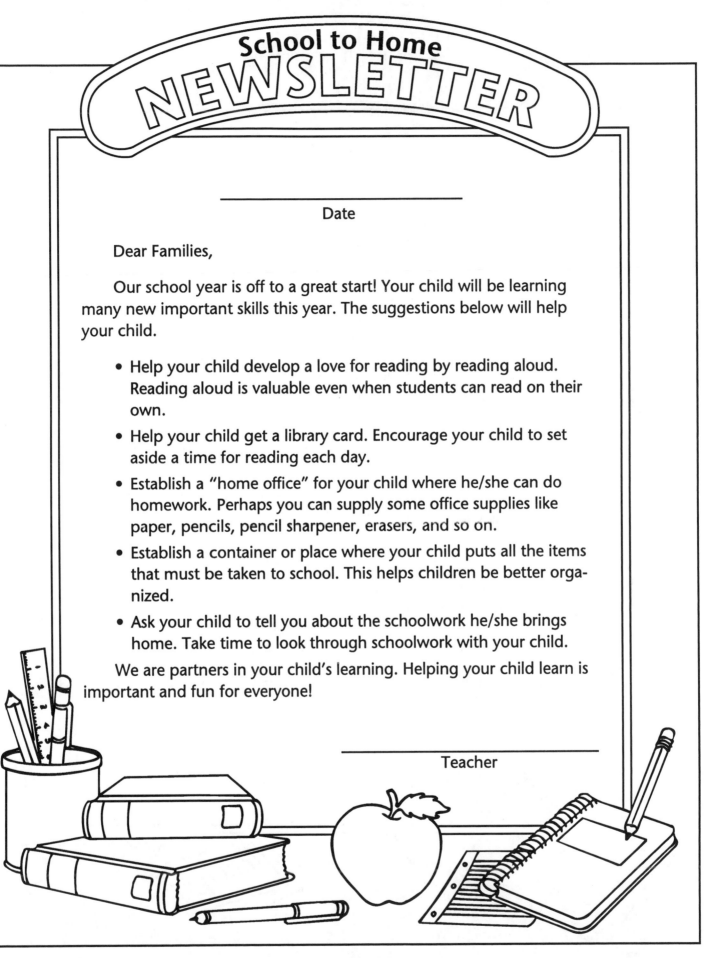

reproducible page

277

FS-8128 *100% Practical*

School to Home NEWSLETTER

_____

Date

Dear Families,

All students benefit from extra reading experiences. Share the joy of reading with your child through these activities.

When you read aloud to your child:

- Stop part of the way through the story and ask your child to predict what will happen next.
- Ask your child how the story made him/her feel.
- After reading the story, ask your child to suggest a different way the story could have ended.

When you go through your mail, let your child open and read advertising mail you do not want.

In the car, read highway signs aloud with your child.

Let your child help you read and prepare a recipe. At the library, look for special cookbooks for children.

Take books along in the car when traveling on errands or vacations.

Reading together is fun! Help your child start reading more today.

_____

Teacher

reproducible page

School to Home
NEWSLETTER

_____
Date

Dear Families,

These fun-to-do math activities will reinforce math skills taught here at school.

- Have students keep track of the number of minutes he/she watches television for one week.

- Let your child use a mail-order catalog and a calculator. Let your child choose three things to buy and add up the cost on paper. Then he/she can check the numbers with the calculator.

- Give your child the itemized receipt from the grocery store and a calculator. Let your child add up the amount you spent on one category of food (dairy products, fruits and vegetables, meats).

- Make sure your child knows how to tell time on a non-digital clock.

- Use pennies, nickels, dimes, and quarters to teach your child about counting money. Teach your child the names of the coins and what they are worth. Make different combinations of coins to equal the same amount of money.

Helping your child learn at home shows that you place a high value on learning.

_____
Teacher

reproducible page
279

School to Home
NEWSLETTER

_____
Date

Dear Families,

Your child will enjoy making gifts to give to others. Next time your child is looking for something to do, you may want to suggest one of these fun-to-do activities.

- **Make Greeting Cards**

  Encourage your child to make greeting cards for friends and relatives.

- **Make a Bank**

  Your child can make a bank from a round oatmeal or salt box, or a coffee can with a plastic lid. Glue fabric, yarn, or stickers to the container.

- **Make Bookmarks**

  Teach your child to braid yarn into bookmarks. Cute bookmarks can also be made from the fronts of used greeting cards.

- **Make a Scrapbook**

  Help your child make a scrapbook about him/herself to give to a relative. It can contain drawings, schoolwork, photographs, and comments from your child.

- **Make a Coupon Book**

  Help your child make a coupon book of helpful things he/she can do for someone.

Your child will enjoy making things for others.

_____
Teacher

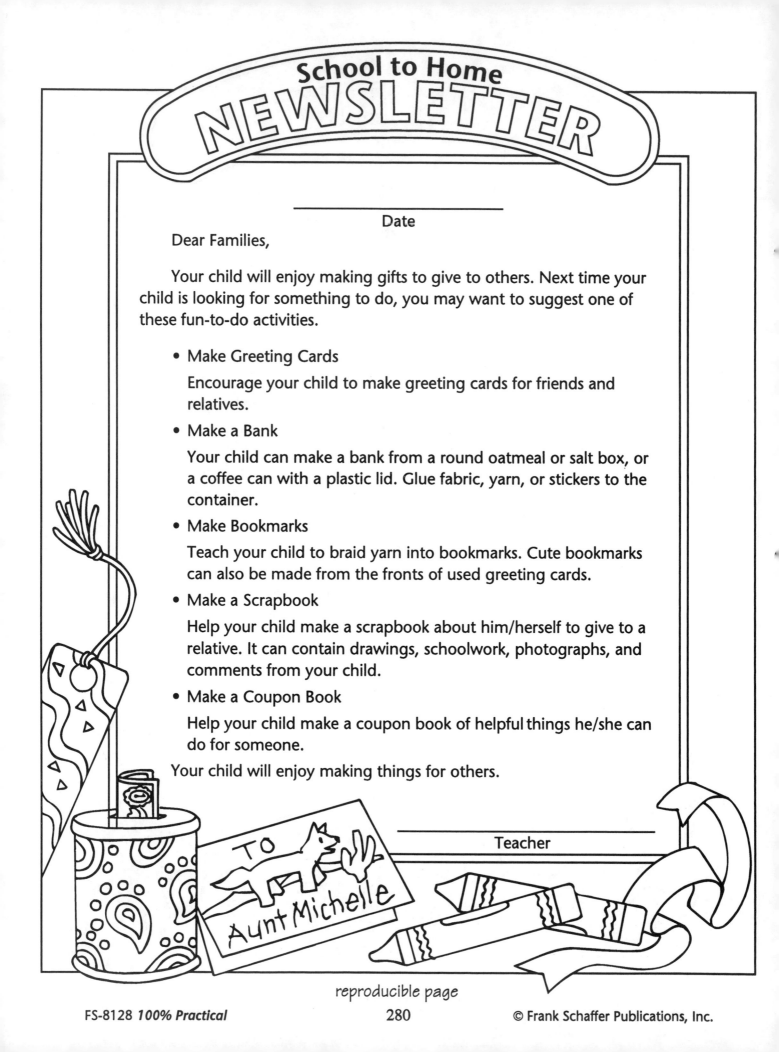

reproducible page

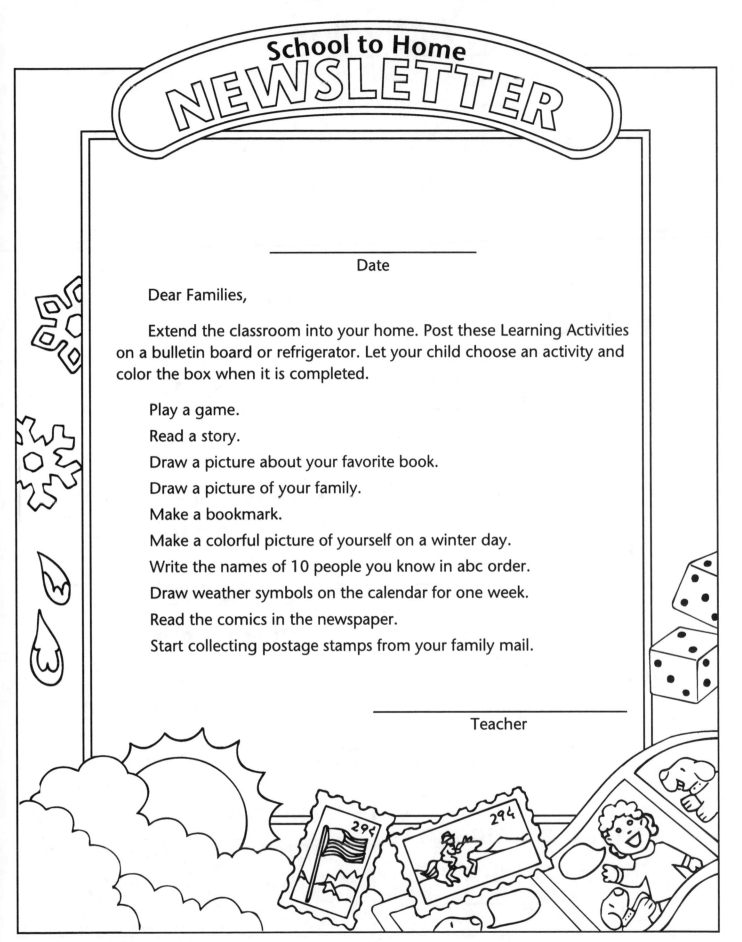

School to Home
NEWSLETTER

_____
Date

Dear Families,

Extend the classroom into your home. Post these Learning Activities on a bulletin board or refrigerator. Let your child choose an activity and color the box when it is completed.

Play a game.

Read a story.

Draw a picture about your favorite book.

Draw a picture of your family.

Make a bookmark.

Make a colorful picture of yourself on a winter day.

Write the names of 10 people you know in abc order.

Draw weather symbols on the calendar for one week.

Read the comics in the newspaper.

Start collecting postage stamps from your family mail.

_____
Teacher

Teacher: Use with page 282.

FS-8128 *100% Practical*

Activities

Play a game.

Read a story.

Draw a picture about your favorite book.

Draw a picture of your family.

Make a book mark.

Make a colorful picture of yourself on a winter day.

Write the names of 10 people you know in abc order.

Draw a symbol for the weather on the calendar for one week.

Read the comics in the newspaper.

Start collecting postage stamps from mail your family receives.

School to Home
NEWSLETTER

_____
Date

Dear Families,

Our days at school are filled with learning activities. I've listed some questions below that you may want to use to start a conversation with your child about school.

1. What do you do when you first get to school?

2. What is your favorite part of the school day?

3. What is the most difficult school subject?

4. What is the easiest subject for you?

5. What do you usually do at recess?

6. Who do you usually eat with at lunchtime?

7. If you could change one thing about school, what would it be?

8. What are you looking forward to at school?

Perhaps you can share some information about your days in elementary school with your child. Conversations about school let your child know that you think school is important and you care about how the year is going.

_____
Teacher

reproducible page
283

FS-8128 *100% Practical*

School to Home
NEWSLETTER

_____
Date

Dear Families,

Parent conferences provide an opportunity for you to learn about your child's progress here at school. These suggestions can help you get the most from our upcoming conference.

- Talk with your child about school. Take a moment to jot down any questions or concerns you want to discuss at our meeting.
- So you can focus on the conference, it is best to avoid bringing younger children to the conference.
- Please come to the conference on time or a few minutes early so you are not feeling rushed.

I'm looking forward to talking with you.

Bring the handy reminder form below to our conference.

_____
Teacher
- -

Conference Day/Date   Time

Teacher's Name   Room #

Questions to ask:

Other concerns:

FS-8128 *100% Practical*   © Frank Schaffer Publications, Inc.

School to Home NEWSLETTER

_____
Date

Dear Families,

It is your child's responsibility to complete homework and to turn it in on time. These tips will help your child develop a sense of responsibility about homework.

- Talk with your child about setting aside a certain time and place for doing homework.

- Don't volunteer to help with homework. Encourage your child to complete the assignment independently. If your child has difficulty with homework, jot a note to me on the homework.

- Help your child be better organized by designating a place where he/she can put the things that need to be taken to school. A box, basket, or dishpan works well for this.

Homework is your child's responsibility. Have your child show you his completed homework assignments so you are aware of the kind of work your child is doing.

_____
Teacher

reproducible page

FS-8128 _100% Practical_

School to Home NEWSLETTER

_____

Date

Dear Families,

Encourage your child to try these writing activities at home. They will help your child understand the value of the writing skills being taught at school.

- Phone Directory

    Perhaps your child can make a little telephone directory of names and phone numbers of friends and relatives he/she is allowed to call.

- Family Notes

    Write notes to your child and tuck them in his/her lunch or on the family refrigerator.

- Help your child write a note to a faraway friend or relative.

- Ask your child to write items the family needs to buy on the grocery-shopping list.

- Provide writing paper, colorful pens and pencils, and stickers to make writing activities fun for your child.

- Have your child add a line to a letter you are writing.

Every child benefits from writing activities.

_____

Teacher

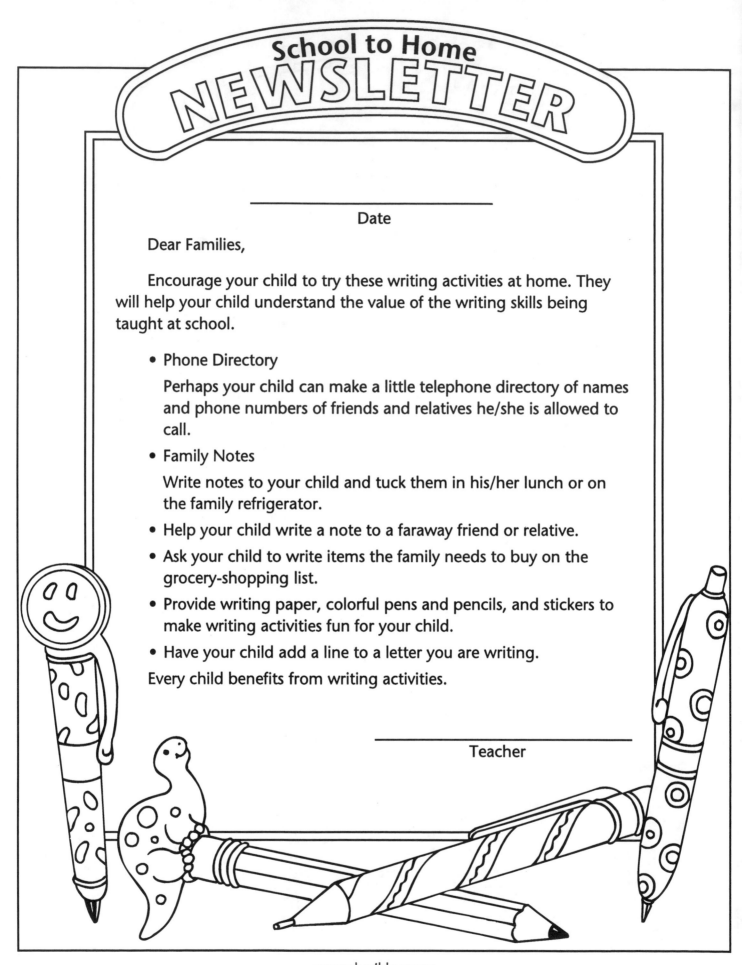

reproducible page

School to Home NEWSLETTER

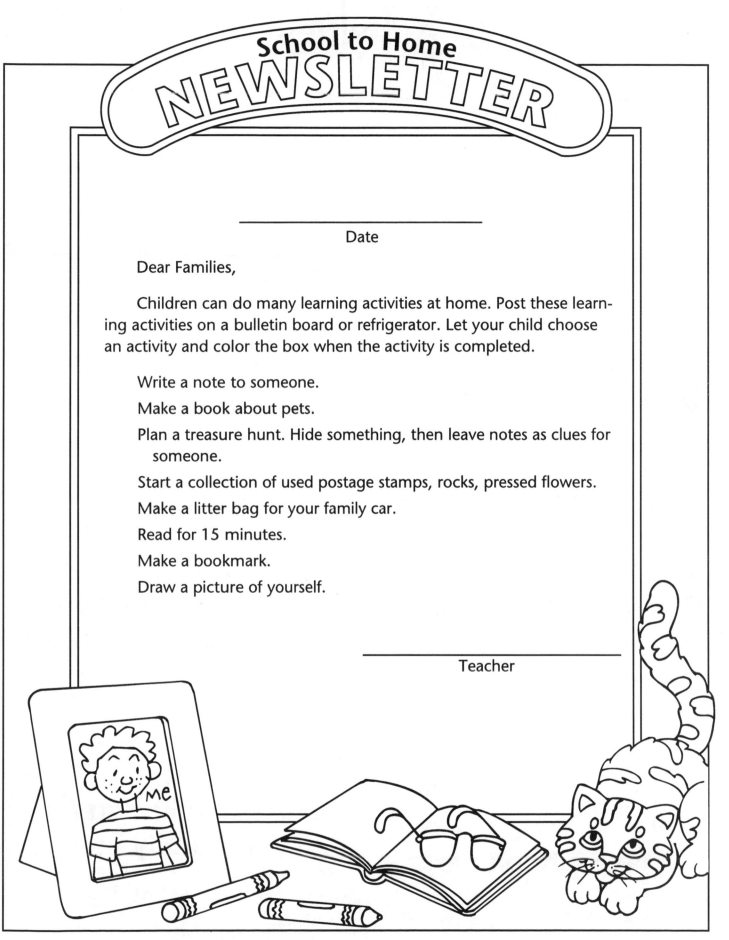

_____
Date

Dear Families,

Children can do many learning activities at home. Post these learning activities on a bulletin board or refrigerator. Let your child choose an activity and color the box when the activity is completed.

Write a note to someone.

Make a book about pets.

Plan a treasure hunt. Hide something, then leave notes as clues for someone.

Start a collection of used postage stamps, rocks, pressed flowers.

Make a litter bag for your family car.

Read for 15 minutes.

Make a bookmark.

Draw a picture of yourself.

_____
Teacher

Teacher: Use with page 288.

reproducible page

Activities

Write a note to someone.

Make a book about pets.

Make a treasure hunt. Hide something, then leave notes as clues for someone.

Make a picture of yourself.

Read for 15 minutes.

Start a collection of used postage stamps, rocks, pressed flowers.

Make a bookmark.

Make a litter bag for your family car.

Teacher: Use with page 287.

reproducible page

Instant Letters for School Families

Additional ready-to-reproduce letters for parents can be found in these chapters:

Chapter 2, "Reading Aloud . . . ," **pages 27–28**

Chapter 8 "Using Themes," **page 154**

Stationery for Teachers

Reproducible writing paper is provided on **pages 290–293**. Use it for communicating with school families and colleagues.

Dear Families,
   We are beginning a theme study on plants. Can you help us by providing any seeds or living plants?
                                                    Mrs. Jackson

Keep family communication ongoing.

You don't have to be an artist to add flair to your communications. Use the predesigned pages!

Open-Ended Decorative Pages

Create your own activities, letters, homework sheets, or anything else you can imagine with the open-ended decorative pages on **pages 295–302**.

Reproduce a copy to write on (so you can save the original to reuse). Fill in the information you want, then reproduce for students. Use and again and again for different activities and purposes.

Frequent communication is appreciated by families and enhances public relations for our schools. Families want to know what is happening at school and also appreciate information from teachers about how to help their children learn.

FS-8128 *100% Practical*

To: _____ From: _____ Date: _____

reproducible page

FS-8128 *100% Practical*

reproducible page

FS-8128 *100% Practical*

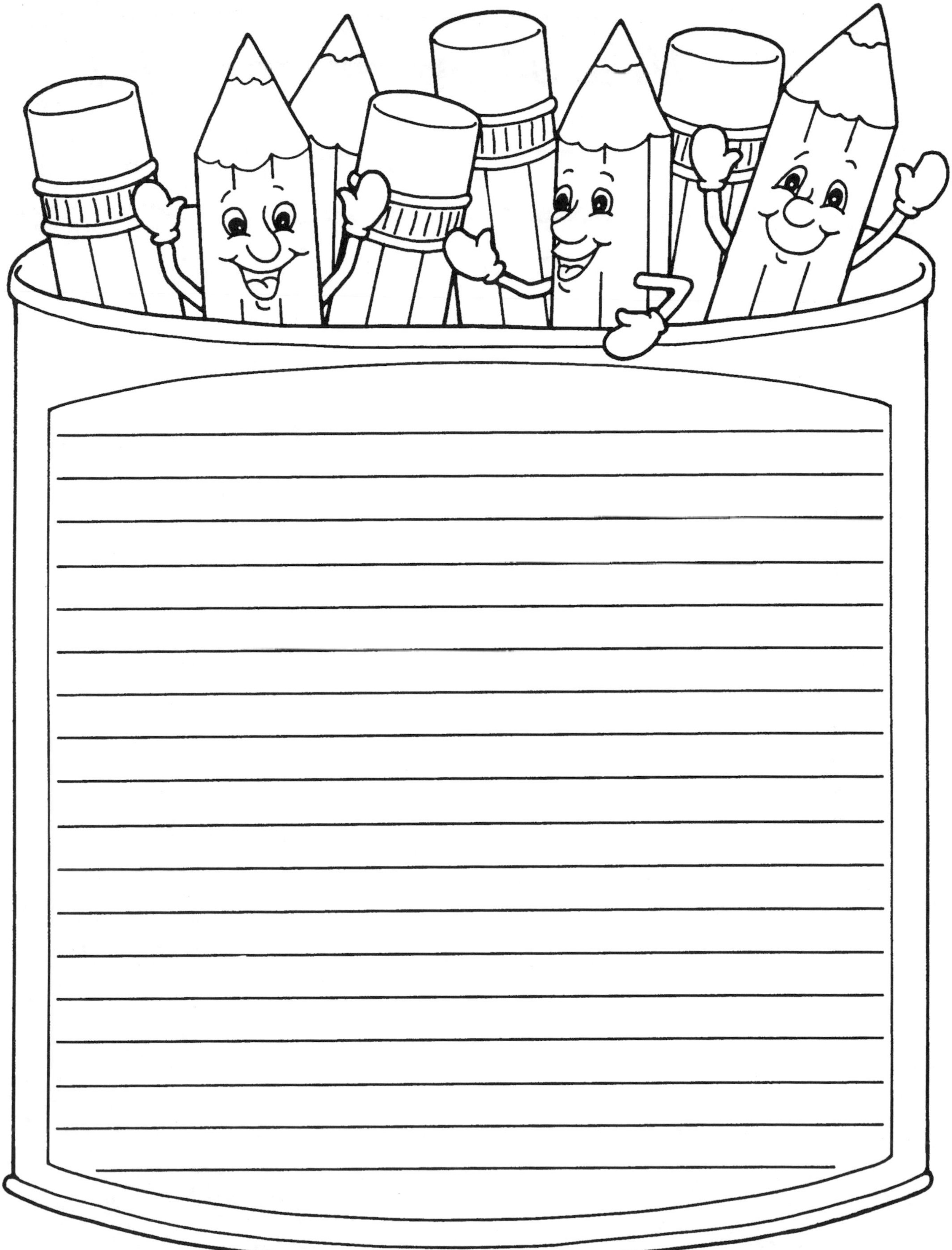

What's Happening

ANNOUNCING . . .

Event _____

Date _____

Time _____

Place _____

Message _____

_____

FS-8128 *100% Practical*

Handy Optopus

FS-8128 *100% Practical*

Big Dino

Pen and Paper

reproducible page
297

FS-8128 *100% Practical*

Look at This!

Spring

FS-8128 *100% Practical*

Summer

FS-8128 *100% Practical*

Autumn

FS-8128 *100% Practical*

Winter

FS-8128 *100% Practical*

NOTES

FS-8128 *100% Practical*

NOTES